*Georges Bataille*

Twayne's World Authors Series
French Literature

David O'Connell, Editor

*Georgia State University*

TWAS 872

GEORGES BATAILLE
*Charpentier/L'Express*

# *Georges Bataille*

Roland A. Champagne

*University of Missouri–St. Louis*

Twayne Publishers
An Imprint of Simon & Schuster Macmillan
New York

Prentice Hall International
London • Mexico City • New Delhi • Singapore • Sydney • Toronto

Twayne's World Authors Series No. 872

*Georges Bataille*
Roland A. Champagne



Twayne Publishers
An Imprint of Simon & Schuster Macmillan
1633 Broadway
New York, NY 10019

**Library of Congress Cataloging-in-Publication Data**

Champagne, Roland A.
Georges Bataille / Roland A. Champagne.
p. cm. — (Twayne's world authors series ; TWAS 872. French literature)
Includes bibliographical references and index.
ISBN 0-8057-7821-7 (alk. paper)
1. Bataille, Georges, 1897–1962 I. Title. II. Series.
III. Series: Twayne's world authors series; TWAS 872. IV. Series:
Twayne's world authors series. French literature.
PQ2603.A695Z627 1998
848'.91209—dc21 98-21555
CIP

This paper meets the requirements of ANSI/NISO Z3948–1992 (Permanence of Paper).

10 9 8 7 6 5 4 3 2 1

Printed in the United States of America

*To Nina and Noah,*
*for their electric smiles in times of extreme anguish*

# *Contents*

# *Preface*

Georges Bataille (1897–1962) did not receive the accolades his work deserved during his lifetime. His writings were published during that period by small presses in France, in the case of his erotic writings under pseudonyms, and not translated abroad except for some of his work, notably his essays on art and the drawings in the Lascaux caves. During the 1960s, Philippe Sollers, Michel Foucault, and the Tel Quel Group in Paris revived his work through their own essays as well as conferences on his work and the publication of those proceedings. Thanks to the tenacious resolve of Denis Hollier in beginning the first volume of Bataille's collected works, we now have Bataille's entire opus in 12 volumes, which were published by Gallimard in French from 1970 to 1988. In English, most of his works have also been translated due to the popularity of his ideas to the generation of writer-intellectuals who have come to be known as "poststructuralists." Bataille's work, however, contains a much broader vision for humanity than that attributed to him by the concerns of the poststructuralists. I present here the overall scale of his work through an exposure of its five major components: his biography, the influences on his work, an overview of the "general economy" of his writings, the appropriations of his writings by major intellectuals, and the overlooked affirmations of Bataille.

Chapter 1 presents Bataille's life centered around his presentation of "atheology," a discussion of the sacred that is not God-centered. I divide his life into five periods, beginning with his conversion to Christianity (1897–1922), followed by the aegis of surrealism (1922–1929), continuing in his organization of the College of Sociology (1930–1939), elaborating the war years (1940–1945), and ending with his withdrawal from politics into literary ventures (1946–1962).

Chapter 2 examines the major influences, what I call inclinations, in Bataille's writings. These influences on his work are organized generally along the lines of traces from Sade, Nietzsche, Hegel, Durkheim, Mauss, Marx, Weber, Pascal, and Unamuno. Each of these writers continued to have an effect on Bataille's writings. More than merely being influenced by one or the other at a certain stage of his life, Bataille was inclined toward their orientations in the spiraling manner that Giambattista Vico ascribed to history in 1744.

Bataille's lifework is presented according to his own admission of having more than one face. Chapter 3 is organized in six sections according to the genres of his work, how I interpret the "faces" or facets of his writing: his creative fiction, his poetry, his essays, his journal editing, his politics, and his scientific pretensions.

Bataille's work has become increasingly significant in varying ways to commentators on twentieth-century cultural forces. In chapter 4, there are five sections that recount how groups of intellectuals have appropriated parts of Bataille's writings for their own agendas. Beginning with André Breton's arguments against Bataille and for Breton's vision of surrealism, I then discuss how Maurice Blanchot and Jean-Paul Sartre evaluated Bataille's work, basically during and immediately after World War II. The third section on Bataille's influence reviews the arguments of Philippe Sollers, Denis Hollier, Roland Barthes, and Susan Sontag presenting Bataille for poststructuralist readers during the late 1960s and early 1970s. Following closely upon the Tel Quel elaborations of Bataille, Jacques Derrida and Jürgen Habermas include Bataille in the elaboration of attitudes about deconstruction. Last, the interests of sociology, through the voices of Jean Baudrillard and Michael Richardson, have included Bataille and receive the attention of the fifth section discussing Bataille's major inroads.

The importance of Bataille's writings is not exhausted by my limited discussion of the major schools he has influenced. The positive thrusts of Bataille's work have many elaborations yet to be made because of the struggles and complexity of his varied interests. Chapter 5 proposes five additional affirmations made in his writings that have been overlooked and could be developed.

I also append a lexicon of Bataille's most common terms. Despite my respect for Denis Hollier's scholarship and his view that it is not possible to isolate the sense of Bataille's changing vocabulary, what he calls "a kind of verbal potlatch,"[1] I have digested for the reader my sense of what Bataille means in the crucial terms with which he struggles. These terms are found in bold text throughout my presentation. I thus offer the benefit of my studies of his complete works and most of the secondary sources.

Although most of Bataille's work is available in English, the translations are unequal in quality and differ in their translations of the same words and terms. In this presentation, unless I indicate a particularly felicitous translation, I myself translate the French into English. Regarding my deliberate uses of the past and present tenses of the verbs in my presentation, present tense refers to what Bataille says in his writings and the past tense to events during his lifetime.

# *Acknowledgments*

I am not alone in this venture. Many have helped me along the way in the experience of reading Bataille. I thank Michel Pierssens for introducing me to Bataille in Vichy, France, and for my first enlightening discussions of Bataille with him and Josette Féral. I appreciate Brian Vandenberg's insights into Bataille and the war as well as his help with *Histoire de l'oeil,* his discussions, and his patience with my sometimes undirected enthusiasm for Bataille. And thanks to Noah, who reminded me one day that "bataille" means "battle" and that above all this book should be about the conflicts and struggles of that namesake.

Books have been generously provided to me by Sally Dobson, Mary Ann Corbett, Sandy Schnell, Mary Doran, Connie Quinlan, Mary Zettwoch, and Lucinda Williams.

The thoughtful reading and suggestions provided by the staff of Impressions Book & Journal Services have been especially helpful.

# *Chronology*

1897 Georges Bataille born on 10 September in Billom, Puy-de-Dome, as the second of two sons to Marie-Antoinette (Tournadre) Bataille and the syphilitic Joseph-Aristide Bataille.

1899 Family moves to Reims.

1900 Syphilitic and blind father suffers general paralysis.

1914 Receives his baccalauréat from the Collège d'Epernay; he and his mother leave his father behind during the seige of Reims and flee to Rion-ès-Montagnes; Bataille is formally converted to the Catholic faith in August.

1915 Receives second baccalauréat (philosophy) in June; his father dies in Reims on 6 November.

1916 In January, Bataille is mobilized; he suffers tuberculosis and is released from the military.

1917 Joins the seminary of Saint-Flour to be a priest or a monk.

1918 Writes the pious, six-page article "Notre Dame de Rheims"; leaves the seminary in the fall; on 8 November, Bataille enters the École Nationale des Chartes (the National School of Paleography and Library Science); Bataille's mother moves to Paris and lives with her two sons.

1919 "Notre Dame de Rheims" is published.

1920 Meets Henri Bergson in the British Museum in London; Bataille's pious vocation in the seminary supposedly lost at the French Benedictine Quarr Abbey on the Isle of Wight.

1922 Submits a thesis on "The Order of Chivalry in the Thirteenth Century" and graduates from the École Nationale des Chartes; accepts a fellowship (because Bataille is second in his graduating class) to the School of Advanced Hispanic Studies in Madrid; he travels extensively in southern Spain; he studies the languages of Russian and Tibetan; on 7 May, he witnesses the death of the bullfighter Manolo Granero in Madrid; obtains a position in numismatics at the Bibliothèque Nationale in Paris.

1923–1925 Becomes a philosophy student of Leon Chestov, from whom he learns to read Nietzsche; with Chestov, he translates into French *The Idea of Goodness in Tolstoy and Nietzsche;* Chestov introduces him to Maurice Heine; he is associated with dadaism; he frequents bordellos in Paris and leads a dissolute life.

1924 Jacques Lavaud, a colleague at the BN, introduces Bataille to Michel Leiris and Theodore Fraenkel; proposes the movement *Oui* (Yes) to oppose the extreme negativism of the dadaists.

1925 Contributes anonymously a translation of absurd medieval poems to the surrealist organ *La Révolution surréaliste;* Adrien Borel gives Bataille the photographs of the "torture of 100 forms of punishment"; Leiris brings Bataille to meet André Masson in the latter's studio; meets Antonin Artaud.

1926 Writes a short book, *W. C.,* and later destroys it.

1927 On recommendation of D. Dausse, Bataille is psychoanalyzed by Adrien Borel; he participates in political demonstrations for Sacco and Vanzetti; he writes *L'Anus solaire,* to be published in 1931 accompanied by Masson's etchings.

1928 Marries Sylvia Maklès; *L'Histoire de l'oeil* published under the pseudonym of Lord Auch.

1929 Bataille becomes the general secretary and eventually the editor of the journal *Documents;* Breton's *Deuxième Manifeste du Surréalisme* excoriates Bataille et al.

1930 Bataille and 11 of his colleagues respond to Breton with the pamphlet *Un Cadavre;* on the same day (15 January), Bataille's mother dies; he joins Boris Souvarine's anti-Stalinist *Cercle Communiste Démocratique*; Bataille's daughter Laurence is born to his wife Sylvia (Maklès).

| | |
|---|---|
| 1931 | Wildenstein withdraws finances for *Documents* because it is a financial loss; close friendship with Raymond Queneau; he meets Colette Peignot (Laure); Bataille contributes to *La Critique sociale* until 1934. |
| 1932–1933 | Names and establishes the journal *Minotaure,* which later belongs to the surrealists. |
| 1933 | With René Lefebvre Bataille founds *Masses,* a seminar to discuss socialist issues between intellectuals and workers; essays on expenditure in *La Critique sociale;* Bataille begins attending lectures by Alexandre Kojève at the École Pratique des Hautes Études and learns Hegel from him until 1939. |
| 1934 | Meets Roger Caillois at the home of Jacques Lacan. |
| 1934–1938 | Has an ongoing affair with Colette Peignot (Laure) and separation from his wife Sylvia. |
| 1935 | Organizes with Roger Caillois *Contre-Attaque,* a surrealist political activist group that is antifascist, leftist, and communist in spirit; reconciliates with André Breton. |
| 1936 | The collapse of *Contre-Attaque* (Jan.); Bataille flirts with fascism and its tendencies toward violence against the bourgeois world; with Pierre Klossowski and André Masson, Bataille founds the journal *Acéphale* (four issues from 1936 to 1939) dedicated to the work of Nietzsche; Bataille and his wife Silvia (Maklès) appear in Renoir's film *Une Partie de campagne;* writes *Le Bleu du ciel* but delays having it published until 1957; in May, the only issue of *Cahiers de Contre-Attaque* appears; Bataille gives lectures in Jean Wahl's *Collège de philosophie* until 1937; Bataille claims to have spilled blood at the Place de la Concorde and to have placed a skull there in memory of Louis XVI; Bataille visits Masson in Spain and asks him to sketch the Acéphale deity. |
| 1937 | With Roger Caillois and Jules Monnerot, Bataille organizes in March the *Collège de Sociologie,* against traditional science, with meetings every two weeks in the Catholic bookstore Galeries du Livre beginning on 20 November; Bataille also founds the secret society *Acéphale;* Bataille and Colette climb the volcano of Mount Etna. |

1938 Begins the practice of yoga; organizes the "Société de psychologie collective"; Colette Peignot dies at age 35 on 7 November of tuberculosis; Patrick and Isabelle Waldberg move in with Bataille.

1939 Last meeting of the *Collège de Sociologie* on 4 July; begins writing *Le Coupable.*

1940 Meets Maurice Blanchot.

1941 *Madame Edwarda* published under the pseudonym Pierre Angélique.

1942 Recurrent bouts with tuberculosis; he leaves his position at the Bibliothèque Nationale and Paris to retire in Vézeley until 1948; September/October in Normandy with Denise Rollin.

1943 Publishes *L'Expérience intérieure;* meets Diane Kotchoubey de Beauharnais (Mme. Snopko).

1944 Meets often with Jean-Paul Sartre.

1945 Publishes *Sur Nietzsche;* Jules Monnerot's *La poésie moderne et le sacré* is published.

1946 Returns to Paris; he founds the journal *Critique* and is editor of a special issue of *Actualité* on "Espagne libre"; he is divorced from Sylvia Maklès.

1947 Contributes "The Absence of Myth" to *Le Surréalisme en 1947,* a catalogue of a surrealist exhibit on myth; he publicly supports the Marshall Plan.

1948 Daughter Julie is born on 1 December to Bataille and Diane de Beauharnais; Jules Monnerot reveals, to the displeasure of Bataille, that Bataille is the author of *Madame Edwarda* and *L'Histoire de l'oeil.*

1949 Becomes librarian in Charpentras; *La Part maudite* is published.

1950 The novel *L'Abbé C.* is published.

1951 Marries Diane Kotchoubey de Beauharnais on 16 January; he is in charge of the municipal library of Orléans.

1955 His essays on Manet and on the cave drawings of Lascaux are published.

1956 He is a witness in the pornography trial of Jean-Jacques Pauvert for the publication of the Marquis de Sade's work.

1957 *Le Bleu du ciel, La Littérature et le mal,* and *L'Erotisme,* and the third edition of *Madame Edwarda* with his introduction, are published.

1959 *Le Procès de Gilles de Rais* is published.

1961 Publishes *Les Larmes d'Eros,* which is placed on the index of forbidden books by the Roman Catholic Church.

1962 On 8 July, Bataille dies in the company of Jacques Pimpanneau.

1966 *Ma Mère* is published.

# *Chapter One*

# A Biography of Atheology (1897–1962)

Georges Bataille's Catholicism was always with him despite the overt tendencies otherwise in his writings. His erotic narratives, his base materialism (**le matérialisme**), and his concentration upon death and evil all appear to leave behind the idealist focus of Catholicism. However, the shadow of Catholicism stalked Bataille to such an extent that his longtime friend Pierre Klossowski's comments to Bataille after a lecture in 1948 have a haunting ring: "I have found you Catholic at certain moments."[1] Those certain moments were crucial in Bataille's "atheology" (**l'athéologie**), a theory of respect for the sacred (**le sacré**) that excludes God. Bataille thought Klossowski's assertion untenable and did not defend the search for alternatives to the theological doctrines that made Catholicism an idealist label.

Despite Bataille's cold shoulder to Klossowski, Catholicism remained with Bataille after his religious conversion in 1914. When World War II occasioned an abrupt halt to Bataille's political activism in 1939, he experimented with mysticism (**le mysticisme**), having begun practicing yoga in 1938. He tried to distinguish what he called his "inner experiment" from the Catholic mysticism of John of the Cross and Teresa of Avila. This inner experiment (**l'expérience intérieure**) brought him to ecstatic confrontations with eroticism and death (**l'Erotisme, la mort**), which he came to see as means of communication with a community (**la communication, la communauté**) rather than the transcendental conduit to God claimed by Catholic mystics. His father's slow, excruciating death by syphilis (1915), Bataille's exposure to the deaths of war in a military hospital (1916), and Colette Peignot's death by tuberculosis in 1938 made Bataille especially sensitive to Death as the touchstone of the religious nature of his life, but this religion was atheological, that is, by definition without God.

During Bataille's early childhood, his parents did not practice any specific religious faith. When Bataille was about a year old, the family moved from Auvergne to Reims, and his childhood was spent in the looming shadow of the Cathedral of Reims. Against this ever-present backdrop, Bataille converted to Catholicism in 1914 and entered the seminary of Saint-Flour to pursue a religious vocation. During his year in the seminary (1917–1918), he wrote a pious six-page article entitled "Notre Dame de Rheims," a fervent prayer to the Virgin, whose namesake, the cathedral of Reims, had been set ablaze when the German army invaded the town. Many of his critics dismiss this piece as out of character with his later interests. However, his piety was crucial to his interest in the sacred and the nature of myth (**le mythe**) evident throughout his writings. Bataille seriously considered a religious vocation during this time. He would later claim to have lost this calling to the religious life in 1920 on the Isle of Wight when a woman cried as he told her about his Catholicism. These tears, not unlike those he would ascribe to the area of nonknowledge (**le non-savoir**, OC, VIII, 218–19), made him aware of his own body and its denial by Catholicism, especially within the vocation of the monastic or priestly (**le prêtre**) life and its vow of chastity. This aspect of Catholicism is a far cry from the eroticism that would dominate Bataille's life, embodied in his womanizing and his frequent association with prostitutes.

The myths of Catholicism appear throughout Bataille's writings. A myth is a story that a community tells about itself. But for Bataille, myth is not simply a narrative. Ritual is part of the nature of myth because the practices of groups, such as the use of sacrifice (**le sacrifice**), often reveal what is sacred to the group. Catholicism provided Bataille with a point of departure as well as a point of reference for examining how the religious instinct survives even while God becomes extinct (i.e., "God is dead," as Nietzsche announced). Bataille constantly developed the social parameters of the sacred, which had its roots in the theological doctrines of Catholicism. His professional education at the École Nationale des Chartes in Paris from 1918 to 1922 was especially crucial because his thesis on the thirteenth-century order of chivalry opened up to him a network of secular and religious engagements in philosophy, economics, anthropology, mysticism, art history, poetry, and pornography.

The word pornography literally means "writing about prostitutes." Bataille delved into this topic with vigor. He answered the call of the female prostitute and even described his thinking as a prostitute undressing (OC, V, 200). Thus, Bataille's vocation was no saintly calling to Catholicism. Typically he was drawn toward paradox, especially the tension between taboo and transgression (**le tabou, la transgression**).

He had mystical visions of ecstatic moments. However, his mysticism was an earthly kind that precluded transcendence and focused instead on the delights of desire and its satisfaction.

Georges Bataille was probably the first professional French writer to be psychoanalyzed. His analyst, Dr. Adrien Borel, employed the unorthodox method of showing Bataille pictures of a torture victim in order to awaken Bataille to his own problems with guilt, suffering, and violence. The "100 forms of punishment" photographs were taken in 1905 by Georges Dumas and depicted Fou-Tchou Lin being punished for having killed a prince in China. Borel gave these photographs to Bataille in 1925; the memory of them would haunt Bataille for the rest of his life as he examined the practices of sacrifice and violence as part of the rites of the sacred throughout history. In Bataille's novel *Ma Mère* (1966), the narrator finds pornographic photographs in his father's study that likewise haunt him and begin his odyssey toward the inevitable taboo of incest.[2]

In his writings, Bataille constantly explored the visual links among sacrifice, violence, and sexual transgression. Once again, Catholicism was looming in the shadows. The crucifixion of Christ and its celebration through the ritual of eating and drinking his transubstantiated body and blood were never very distant from Bataille's memory as examples of human religious rituals uniting the sacred, the dead body, the expenditure (**la dépense**) of energy, base materialism, eroticism, and the communication among the members of a community. A look at the specifics of Bataille's life will show how his religious life became atheological and turned him toward the recognition of the mythical components of Catholicism.

## 1897–1922: Bataille's Parents and His Conversion

Both parents played major roles in the formation of Bataille's ethic of the sacred. When Georges was born in 1897, the second son of 44-year-old Joseph-Aristide Bataille and Marie-Antoinette (Tournadre) Bataille, his father was in the secondary stages of syphilis. He was blind and paralytic during Georges's childhood. Bataille's memory of his father urinating while showing the whites of his eyes (OC, III, 60) suggests both orgasmic delight and Bataille's surrealist image of **l'oeil pinéal** ("the prickly eye"). This is only the first of Bataille's sexual experiences that suggest his father molested him in the basement of their home (OC, II, 10). Haunted by the fear of inheriting his father's disease (OC, III, 61),

Bataille imagined his compulsive writing to be derived from his fear of going mad (OC, VII, 11).

Bataille's mother, Marie-Antoinette, also figured prominently in her son's problems relating to sexuality and madness. Her name recalls the unfortunate wife of Louis XVI, who was beheaded in the Revolution. Bataille would later claim, in 1936, that he placed a skull at the Place de la Concorde and publicly announced that it was Louis XVI's. He also organized a journal (1935) and a secret society (1937) around the title *Acéphale* (**l'Acéphale,** the headless god.) During childhood, Georges felt pity for his mother, whose sexuality is the major topic of his novel *Ma Mère*. Her self-sacrifice to Bataille's syphilitic father is another theme that recurs throughout Bataille's writings. He identifies sacrifice as the highest form of religious experience (OC, X, 183) and explores its implications for the notion of the sacred as well as for the type of communication and the community it engenders. In 1914, during the bombardment of Reims by the Germans in World War I, Bataille's mother escaped with the 16-year-old Georges to her parents' residence in Rion-ès-Montagnes, leaving the paralytic father behind. Bataille would regret having abandoned his father (OC, III, 60), who died during Georges's absence from Reims. Marie-Antoinette would continue to be closely associated with her son until her death in 1930. In 1918, she moved in with Georges and his older brother, Martial, in Paris, where Georges obtained a position at the Bibliothèque Nationale. Later, Martial would deny that either of their parents was ever mad,[3] despite Georges's fantastic stories about their mother's two attempts at suicide. Whether or not Marie-Antoinette suffered from actual madness, the anxiety of syphilis and its threats of madness constantly surrounded Bataille's entire family.

Catholicism also provided Bataille the system against which he thrust his versions of blasphemy, sacrilege (**le sacrilège**), and, above all, scatology (**la scatologie**). Within the rituals of Roman Catholicism, especially the sacrifice of the Mass, Bataille found the means to examine the nature of his self, his family, and his notion of community. Bataille formally converted to the Catholic faith in 1914 during his stay at Rion-ès-Montagnes. There was curious timing in his abandonment of his father in Reims and his decision to become a Catholic. He went through the process of "intellectual scatology" (OC, II, 64) whereby he rejected what he could not immediately assimilate, that is, his sexuality relative to both his father and his mother. While becoming pious in his reflections, Bataille was also intellectual and pursued his second baccalaureate (his first was from the Collège d'Epernay in 1914), this time in philosophy.

The war intervened in Bataille's life once again in 1916 when he was conscripted into the military. The military was only a brief respite, however, because Bataille suffered from tuberculosis and was given a medical discharge. Illness would haunt Bataille throughout his life. Tuberculosis caused Colette Peignot's death in 1938, Bataille's separation from the Bibliothèque Nationale in 1942, and finally his death in 1962. Although Bataille never experienced combat duty, he witnessed firsthand the horrors of the war's effect on humanity as he found himself hospitalized beside soldiers rendered helpless with war wounds. He internalized the war, reflecting that "I myself am at war" (OC, I, 557).

Bataille's internalized war, however, was a religious one. Like Stendhal's Julien Sorel, the contrast between the red and the black—the military and religious life—were the vocations that called out to the young Bataille. The military did broaden his perspective on life, which caused him to question his piety. For him, the military and the Church were in direct confrontation with each other. Bataille would later question the economics of utility (**l'utilité**) and look back upon the ideology of the Church, noting that "everything that was not *useful* for salvation was condemned and rejected" (OC, II, 241). He decided to enter a Roman Catholic seminary at Saint-Flour to become either a priest or a monk. His six-page article "Notre Dame de Rheims," which he wrote while at Saint-Flour, is almost idealist in tone. Bataille lost his idealist faith and left the seminary in the fall of 1918. His identification with the priestly calling would always remain with him,[4] as later in life he provided access to the sacred as a political leader and intellectual adventurer. He also made a brief appearance as a seminarian in Jean Renoir's 1935 film *Une Partie de campagne*. Bataille claimed to have confessed to priests from August 1914 until 1920 (OC, III, 61). His attitude about Catholic priests, however, was complicated by his exposure to the materialism and survival ethic of the military in 1916. Later, in "Eponine" (1949), the prelude to his novel *L'Abbé C.*, Bataille explains that "what attracts me to a priest is surely that which he lacks,"[5] that is, a profane and materialist existence. The character Don Aminado, in Bataille's *Histoire de l'oeil,* first published under the pseudonym of Lord Auch in 1928, is desacralized as a priest: he is raped, forced to commit sacrileges against the transubstantiated host and the transmuted wine, and murdered; his dead body is then subjected to atrocities. In the company of a blasphemous trio of licentious young people, the priest is made to recognize his sexuality, his mortality, his potential for transgressing the sacred, and ultimately the base materialism of his being. Bataille thus saw the priest incarnating religion as a ritual that artificially separated the sacred from the profane. He would fuse them back together without rejecting religion.

In 1920, Bataille visited London and met the French philosopher Henri Bergson in the British Museum. This encounter inspired Bataille to read Bergson's work on laughter (**le rire**). Although Bataille was not satisfied with Bergson's exposition, it spurred Bataille's interest in laughter as a means of relieving anxiety and also as the focus of the relationship between body and mind. He would reflect upon laughter, and its importance for him, throughout his writings.

Bataille's relationship with his mother also became increasingly complex during the years following the war. After leaving the seminary, he entered the École Nationale des Chartes in Paris in 1918. He moved into the apartment of his older brother Martial, followed shortly by their mother. Georges's complex desires concerning his mother are revealed in the erotic and ultimately incestuous relationship between the narrator and his mother in *Ma Mère*. In this novel, the narrator's father dies, leaving the mother to educate her son in sexual matters. She uses pornographic pictures; other women, including her own lesbian lovers; and finally herself to complete her son's introduction to sexuality. There is no verification that such a relationship existed during Bataille's lifetime. Nevertheless, in Paris Bataille began a period of experimentation, both sexual and intellectual. His mother's presence must have been the source of at least some of the anxiety that fills all his creative work.

After meeting Bergson in London and leaving his pious thoughts behind on the Isle of Wight in 1920, Bataille submitted his thesis on the order of chivalry in the thirteenth century, graduated from the École des Chartes, and received a fellowship to study in Madrid, giving him the opportunity to travel extensively in Spain.[6] He also witnessed the death of the bullfighter Manolo Granero on 7 May 1922, an incident that figures in *L'Histoire de l'oeil* and probably his essay "L'oeil pinéal" as death graphically reminds him of his father's blind eyes and the sexuality that he tried to ignore during his pious years (1914–1920). The bullfight itself, as Michel Leiris discusses in his own work and probably discussed with the young Bataille, reminds Bataille that ". . . a cathedral is still, impoverished by its Christian disparagement, only a distant invocation of long-established festivals" (OC, VII, 224). Pagan rituals were shadows that placed the cathedral itself in a shadow. The sun, worshipped by the Aztecs as well as other pagan cultures, replaces the cathedral in Bataille's mind as the obsessive symbol. The sun, so omnipresent in

Spain, represents the expenditure of energy that is also exhibited by the power of the bull in the Spanish bullfight. Both these representations appear in Bataille's fiction. During Bataille's sojourn in Spain, he observed that the matador was usually skillful at maneuvering the energy of the bull. However, there were moments of uncontrolled violence by the bull, as in the death of Granero, witnessed by Bataille and reiterated in his writings. The bullfight thus becomes a ritual of the bullfighter Granero's sacrifice for the acknowledgment of the absolute rule of power and energy in the universe. Typically, the bullfight entails the ritual killing of the bull just as ancient religious rituals of sacrifice entailed the killing of a calf. However, the Granero experience caused Bataille to rethink the notion of sacrifice, so symbolically important to the Roman Catholic ritual of the Mass. He notes: "The fact of saying certain words over a piece of bread is every bit as satisfying for the spirit as the slitting of a cow's throat" (OC, VIII, 194). Bataille's religious concerns began to be less focused on God as the sacred principle behind sacrifice and more on the human emotions that generate the need for ritual and sacrifice. As he says in a letter written later to René Char, "We have known for a long time that nothing can be found in God that we cannot find in ourselves."[7] His sojourn in Spain suggested to him a more materialistic, less idealistic sense of religion.

Miguel de Unamuno's *The Tragic Sense of Life* appeared in 1913 in Spain. Unamuno had been raised a devout Roman Catholic and had experienced a religious crisis in 1897. Although there is no record that Bataille met Unamuno during his first trip to Spain, it is very likely that Unamuno's work was available for Bataille's perusal. Unamuno has many concerns similar to those of the later Bataille. Unamuno focuses on the struggle of the believer faced with "atheologians" and the anguish and suffering of skepticism in the "depths of the abyss **(l'abîme)**"[8] as well as the importance of mysticism (he calls it "beatific vision") for an ethic of "mutual imposition," Unamuno's term for the religious role of social acts. Understood traditionally, Unamuno provides a justification for a skeptical outlook on the "absurd" with a philosophical outlook that links Friedrich Schleiermacher (1768–1834) and Søren Kierkegaard (1813–1855) with the Existentialists. Bataille adds yet another dimension, base materialism, to ground Unamuno's mysticism in eroticism and to provide a human vision for atheology. Despite this coincidence of themes and the timing of Bataille's visit to Spain corresponding to that of the publication of Unamuno's major works, neither Bataille nor any of his major critics has acknowledged Unamuno's role in Bataille's crisis of faith upon his return from Spain. Meanwhile, Paris called out to him to explore the nature of that inner experience.

## 1922–1929: The Aegis of Surrealism

In 1922, Bataille received an appointment in Paris at the Bibliothèque Nationale (BN) as a numismatist, a curator of its medals and coins division. In Paris, intellectual issues were centered around the audacious avant-garde challenges presented by Tristan Tzara's dadaism and André Breton's surrealism. Bataille's fate would soon be enmeshed in these issues. Before becoming a fellow traveler in these avant-garde ventures, Bataille began reading Nietzsche as a student of Leon Chestov, focusing on the death of God and its implications upon the heels of Pascal, Kierkegaard, and Dostoyevsky. Through Jacques Lavaud, a colleague at the BN, Bataille met Michel Leiris and Theodore Fraenkel. Leiris notes that in 1924, Bataille launched into a period of debauchery, frequenting the nightclubs and bordellos of Paris. This behavior is distinct from his pious ways that Bataille's associates still observed in 1922. By 1924, Bataille also began to be concerned with a dapper appearance, sporting a grey hat and herringbone towncoat at the moment of his introduction to Leiris[9] as well as a bamboo-handled umbrella (OC, V, 46–47) when meeting André Breton.

Fraenkel, Leiris, and Bataille discussed Leiris's excitement about surrealism and the current trends in Paris. Dadaism was too predictable for Bataille in its constant use of "no." Bataille proposed an alternative movement named "yes" (*Oui*) that would affirm life rather than reject lifestyles. Bataille's position regarding surrealism was complex. While his French biographer, Michel Surya, claims that Bataille simply judged surrealism to be fraudulent (Surya, 92), Michael Richardson presents a much more convincing case that many of surrealism's concerns, such as the roles of myth and the sacred in poetry, would return to become central to Bataille's thought from 1945 to 1951.[10] The authoritarian leadership of André Breton in surrealism, however, was troubling to Bataille during the 1920s. Despite his reservations about what Breton was doing, Bataille contributed in 1925 a translation of a medieval document to the surrealist journal *La Révolution surréaliste*.

Meanwhile, in 1925 Georges Bataille became the first major French writer to be psychoanalyzed. His analyst, Adrien Borel, chose an unorthodox approach by presenting Bataille with photographs taken in 1905 by Georges Dumas of the "100 forms of punishment" meted out to Fou-Tchou Lin in China for the murder of Prince Ao Han Ouan. The violence and extreme cruelty depicted in these photographs recur throughout Bataille's writings as ways to depict his own anxieties, dating back to his father's syphilitic eyes and his mother's suicidal tendencies and forward to his interests in atheological rituals and mystical visions. Bataille also studied the Tibetan language during this period. The Chinese origins of these photographs may be linked to Bataille's focus on Oriental mysticism (Zen Buddhism, tantric religion, ecstatic visions (**l'extase**), and, later, yoga). All of these concerns suggest that his psychoanalysis only began with Borel and may never have been completed. His continual interest in religion and inner experiments throughout his life attest to his search for relief from the anxieties that plagued him long before Borel introduced the disturbing photographs.

During the mid 1920s, Bataille also met André Masson and Antonin Artaud. Masson contributed artwork to Bataille's early erotic writings and would join Bataille in marrying into the Maklès family. Artaud, also an erstwhile surrealist, would during the 1960s become celebrated by the Tel Quel Group and Philippe Sollers as having inspired France's avant-garde writers.

Through Masson and Fraenkel, Bataille met Sylvia Maklès, and the two married in 1928. She was an actress and the oldest of four sisters who each married intellectuals (Rose to André Masson, Bianca to Theodore Fraenkel, Simone to Jean Piel; Sylvia also married Jacques Lacan after her divorce from Bataille). The story of the Maklès sisters in the 1930s is certainly a subject deserving of attention.[11] Despite his marriage to Sylvia, Bataille was unrestrained in his philandering. He was never what one could call a faithful spouse.

In the same year he was married, Bataille's pornographic short story, *Histoire de l'oeil*, was published under the pseudonym of Lord Auch. The story is about the education of a trio of adolescents who together act out their sexual fantasies. It resembles Bataille's own anxieties and concerns he felt during his trip to Spain. Likewise, the story reflects the problems that his psychoanalysis may have brought to light regarding his relationships with his father and his mother as well as questions about authority, suffering, and violent changes in behavior. Since the story was published after his psychoanalysis, Bataille by that time might have obtained enough distance from his anxieties to portray the humor in his youthful male narrator trying to act out the implications of his repressed fears and doubts in his relationships with others.[12]

The art world also beckoned to Bataille during the 1920s. The art collector Georges Wildenstein founded the journal *Documents* in 1929 and appointed Bataille its secretary-general. Bataille eventually became the journal's editor. In *Documents*, Bataille published many of his own essays as well as articles by erstwhile surrealists who had become disenchanted with André Breton's leadership. In this journal, Bataille explored the relationships between the visual and the textual. His interest in art remained strong throughout his career. In 1955, he published books on the paintings of Manet and the Lascaux cave drawings[13] as interests that question authority through rituals and visual experiments. Meanwhile, André Breton, the leader of surrealism, was threatened by Bataille's work in *Documents*. In the *Second Manifesto on Surrealism* in 1929, Breton retaliates by attacking Bataille for organizing a countermovement with a base materialism. This commentary began a new stage in Bataille's career.

## 1930–1939: Political Activism and the Birth of a College

In 1930, Bataille and 11 of his newfound colleagues responded to Breton by publishing a pamphlet entitled *Un Cadavre,* a pun on the 1924 surrealist pamphlet against Anatole France.[14] This time, however, Breton was the recipient of the wrath as he was mocked for his pseudoreligious vocabulary and his pompous, narrow leadership based on his readings of Marx and Freud. Breton responded in subsequent manifestos on surrealism by excoriating Bataille for trying to replace surrealism with a substitute movement. The exchange alienated Breton from Bataille and was responsible for the assumption by many critics that Bataille set himself off against surrealism.

Bataille's ties to surrealism, however, were more profound than his dispute with Breton indicated. Despite the rift between Bataille and Breton in 1929 and 1930, Bataille reconciled with Breton in 1935 to organize a surrealist antifascist group (*Contre-Attaque*) and formally reallied himself with surrealism in 1947. In addition, since the early 1920s, Bataille demonstrated interests similar to those of the surrealists in art (he often included André Masson's sketches with his essays and creative writing), religion (he was fascinated by the cult of sacrifice and its ritualistic practice by heterogeneous cultural groups), the unconscious (he entered into psychoanalysis), non-Western mythology (he was a numismatist at the BN), and politics (in 1927, he participated in political demonstrations for Sacco and Vanzetti as he was convinced that democracy was impotent in combatting fascism[15]). His short story *L'Histoire de l'oeil*, written in 1928 and rewritten several times thereafter, can also be read as an exploration of his surrealist interests.

More pointedly, *Un Cadavre* presented an opportunity for Bataille. He wanted to be the leader of a group; he was not comfortable following the agenda of another intellectual. He was interested in group dynamics and in the sociology of religion, as discussed in the *Collège de Sociologie,* the series of seminars he, Roger Caillois, and Jules Monnerot sponsored in 1938 and 1939. Although Bataille criticized Breton for his hegemonic influence, Bataille himself was eager to replace Breton as the leader of surrealism and to place himself at center stage culturally in Paris. In 1931, however, Waldenstein withdrew his support for the journal *Documents,* apparently because it was a financial loss, and Bataille's opportunity faded.

On the same day of the publication of *Un Cadavre* in 1930, Bataille's mother died. His journal has a curious entry regarding this moment: "Thank God, my mother is dead. I am freed from the lie, from the hand capable of helping. My mother is dead, she who stifled."[16] One wonders about the nature of "the lie." Perhaps it was that she was capable of protecting him from death, of being his buffer since she should normally die first. It may also have been more complex because of their joint abandonment of Bataille's father in Reims and her role as the buffer between Georges and his memory of who and what his father was. The mother's stifling or smothering could be part of Bataille's ongoing anxiety, which occupies such a large role in his writing. Marie-Antoinette's death did produce a sense of freedom in Bataille, especially because 1930 was also the year of his daughter Laurence's birth, giving him a sense of the continuity of life.

Bataille also sought continuity in his political life. He perpetuated his antiauthoritarian politics against Breton by becoming involved in Boris Souvarine's anti-Stalinist *Cercle Communiste Démocratique.* Souvarine also edited the journal *La Critique sociale* as the organ for his ideology. From 1931 to 1934 Bataille contributed essays to this journal, especially his influential reflections on expenditure and the psychological structure of fascism. In this latter essay Bataille exhibits his fascination with fascism. He was attracted by violence and the threat it posed to the corrupt values of capitalist society and the bourgeois world. The themes of many of the lectures of the *Collège de Sociologie* would develop these interests further. Bataille was not a committed fascist, however. Many scholars have been intrigued by this essay and how it fits in with Bataille's overall work.[17] Intellectually, Bataille was intrigued by the alternatives fascism presented, but he never took a stand for its implementation as a political system.[18]

In 1931, through his links with Souvarine, Bataille met Simone Weil, the model for the character Lazare in his novel *Le Bleu du ciel*, and Colette Peignot, who would become his beloved "Laure" and who some thought to be the inspiration for many of Bataille's writings during the 1930s.[19] His liaison with Peignot would continue until her death in 1938. Meanwhile, at the Bibliothèque Nationale, Bataille also met and began an enduring friendship with Raymond Queneau, who made daily visits to the BN.

During the period of 1932 to 1933, Bataille was involved in several aborted efforts. He named and established the journal *Minotaure,* which would later belong to the surrealists. He also collaborated with René Lefebvre to establish *Masses*, a "popular university" or seminar between intellectuals and workers that failed but would become the basis for his launch of the *Collège de Sociologie* with Roger Caillois.[20] Bataille also began attending the lectures of Marcel Mauss on ethnology and Alexandre Kojève on Hegel at the *École Pratique des Hautes Études.* He continued to study Hegel with Kojève until 1939.

In 1934, Bataille began some continuing friendships. He met Roger Caillois at the home of Jacques Lacan, who would later marry Bataille's first wife, Sylvia Maklès. Caillois, along with Jules Monnerot, was a sociologist. Together, they began a program to "expound" what Bataille called "sacred sociology."[21] Michael Richardson would even classify Bataille primarily as a sociologist.[22] Caillois and Bataille were both leaders and liked to control the agendas of the groups with which they were engaged. This common characteristic has led some critics, such as Pierre Klossowski, to speculate that the two "hated each other" (Lévy, 171). However, their relationship was much more complicated than simple hatred would explain. Perhaps love as well as hatred drove them to work together. Nevertheless, in 1935, Bataille and Caillois organized the political activist group *Contre-Attaque.* The group was surrealist, left-wing, and antifascist. Its activities involved Breton but were short-lived. The group published a journal, *Cahiers de Contre-Attaque*, which produced its only issue in May 1936.

In the wake of *Contre-Attaque,* Bataille founded the *Acéphale,* a journal dedicated to the work of Nietzsche, with Pierre Klossowski and André Masson. The group published four issues from 1936 to 1939.

In 1935, Bataille appeared with his wife, Sylvia, in Jean Renoir's film *Une Partie de campagne*. His was a cameo appearance as a seminarian; in real life he was becoming a priestlike mediator in political and intellectual ventures. In the movie, Bataille's character is walking with a group of other clerics and is attracted to Sylvia, who is on a swing nearby. The older priests accompanying him discourage him from looking her way and urge him to continue on his walk. Bataille's struggle with sensuality, his attraction toward Sylvia, his learning to be the mystic/mediator, and his companionship among other *clercs* is captured in Renoir's simple video frame.

The early 1930s was also the period when Bataille wrote his novel *Le Bleu du ciel,* which was not published until 1957. He also began lecturing in Jean Wahl's *Collège de Philosophie* and continued his association with it until 1937.

In March 1937, Bataille again worked with Caillois and Jules Monnerot to organize a college whose agenda was to work against traditional science. They gave it the name *Collège de Sociologie* and proposed to hold meetings, in seminar fashion with guest lecturers, every two weeks. The lectures began on 20 November. The College met in a Catholic bookstore, Galeries du Livre, and attracted intellectuals from throughout Europe, such as Walter Benjamin, Theodor Adorno, and Max Horkheimer. Many of the College's themes would later be developed further in works by the members of this first generation of the Frankfurt School of Theory (e.g., Adorno and Horkheimer's *The Dialectic of the Enlightenment*, 1947). The importance of the notion of the irrational principle of the sacred for the identity of a society, the role of violence in politics, and the process of change and political revolt were among the seminar topics. Bataille and Caillois struggled with each other for the leadership of the *Collège.* While Bataille railed against Caillois for his "total political incompetence,"[23] Bataille's concern with the sacred met some opposition in Leiris, who accused him of lack of rigor in ignoring the principles of sociological method according to Durkheim and Mauss (Lévy, 171). Nevertheless, the biweekly sessions of the *Collège de Sociologie* continued to take place until 4 July 1939, when World War II broke up the community.

Bataille also organized a secret society called *Acéphale* in 1937. He invited as members Georges Ambrosino, Henri Dubief, Georges Duthuit, Pierre Klossowski, Colette Peignot, and Patrick Waldberg. Peignot was the only woman in the clique until her death in 1938, when Isabelle Waldberg took her place. The group performed strange rituals, including the sacrifice of a goat (none of the members would volunteer to be a human sacrifice). The title of the group was the same as that used for the journal on Nietzsche that Bataille edited from 1936 to 1939. It referred to a headless god associated with tantric fertility cults and theoretically alluded to the society's interests in group communication without hierarchical direction. As part of the strange practices of the *Acéphale* group, Bataille claimed to have spilled blood in 1936 at the Place de la Concorde (where Louis XVI was beheaded) in memory of the last French king, who was sacrificed by the Revolution in the name of the new, headless government. The group formed while Bataille was enjoying a reputation for extreme debauchery (Lévy, 182 ff.). Maurice Blanchot, who became Bataille's good friend during the last 20 years of his life, notes that "being linked with *Acéphale* is abandoning oneself and being resigned: being resigned without recompense to a limitless abandon."[24] The sacrificial, erotic, and base material interests of the title *Acéphale* are explored in Bataille's novel *Le Bleu du ciel*, when Dorothea, who wants to keep Henri's sexual prowess and rid herself of his anxiety, says to him: "If only you could lose your head" (OC, III, 168). Of course, there is some irony in this focus on headlessness when one considers Bataille's own need to direct groups and to decide who belonged or could not belong to them. It is curious that back in 1930 Bataille criticized Breton for directing surrealism in this manner. By 1937 to 1938, Bataille had lost sight of his own earlier critique and appeared more concerned with being a priest officiating in the rituals of this secret society than with the memory of headstrong dictatorial control of social interests.

Apparently in keeping with the secret society's rituals in the name of atheology, Bataille's name for his Godless mystical reflections, Bataille and Colette Peignot climbed Italy's Mount Etna in 1937. Along with her poetic mind and a daring sense of pushing accepted limits, Peignot brought to Bataille and the *Acéphale* group an abiding interest in collective guilt and the ritual of sacrifice. The voyage up Mount Etna had sacrificial, even suicidal overtones. Peignot and Bataille returned to write independently about the harrowing nature of the suffering they experienced there together. The suffering brought them closer to death and to the impossibility of nothingness, two obsessions that characterize Bataille's mystical visions of base materialism found in his writings. The romantic voyage to Mount Etna, described by Chateaubriand's René and perpetuated in nineteenth-century French and German poets' obsession with the image of the abyss and the inner anguish it represents, is also a key concept representing the skepticism of Unamuno's religious experience (e.g., *The Tragic Sense of Life*, 1913), which Bataille had probably become acquainted with in the early 1920s. The theme of inner anguish (**l'angoisse**), so common in Bataille's fictional narrators and his own self-portrayal, is often associated with an image of the chasm (the abyss, the hole), the profundity of which both attracts and repels him, as does death itself. Peignot's memoirs, which Bataille edited after her death in 1938 as Laure's *Le Sacré* (1939), also relive the extreme emotional distress of having attained the rim of Mount Etna.

The *Acéphale* group developed a specific program composed of 11 principles. On 4 April 1936 these principles became the by-laws of the group.[25] Basically, the group was to be a community formed to lift guilt, acknowledge the role of decomposition in a positive way, practice asceticism, practice acephalic play, practice perversion, acknowledge the universal nature of all communities, and change the world by affirming the role of aggression in power. During this year, Bataille visited the artist André Masson in Spain and convinced him to make a drawing of the Acéphale deity.[26] So a visual image of this chthonic deity remains as a sort of gnostic ideal for the group.

In 1938, Bataille began the practice of yoga. This is a crucial enterprise because it foreshadowed his mystical interests during the 1940s and later. Within Hinduism, yoga is a search for the ways of truth, and its practice is restricted to men within that religion. Curiously, Bataille also organized—with the three male psychoanalysts Adrien Borel, René Allendy, and Paul Schiff—the Society for Collective Psychology, inspired by Nietzsche, to study group expressions of anguish, nonknowledge, guilt, and suffering.

All these latter interests were shared with Colette Peignot, who compounded these interests in Bataille when she died of tuberculosis at the age of 35 in late 1938. His guilt, suffering, and anguish about her death magnified his obsession with nonknowledge. Peignot's mother wanted a funeral Mass for her daughter, but Bataille threatened to shoot the priest on the altar.[27] There was no Mass and no violence. Eventually, the two hugged over Peignot's casket. Nevertheless, Bataille was devastated by the death of his Laure. The *Acéphale* group lost two of its chief protagonists. The Waldbergs, Patrick and Isabelle, moved in with Bataille to console him.[28] He continued with the *Collège de Sociologie* until late 1939 when he began writing *Le Coupable*. World War II, which had been looming in the background, finally arrived and caused chaos in Bataille's intellectual circles.

## 1940–1945: The War and Mystical Inner Experiments

Along with the breakup of Bataille's social circles, the war years brought devastation to Bataille's political ambitions. In addition, he suffered the death of yet another of his close friends. Maurice Heine, the Sade scholar and confidant to many of Bataille's Nietzschean visions since the Chestov lectures of the early 1920s, died in 1940. Fortunately, Bataille met Maurice Blanchot in 1940, and Blanchot remained his confidant for many years.

The losses of Peignot and Heine within a few years of each other combined with the loneliness of the war years exacerbated what had already become "the inward turn in Bataille's thought"[29] during the period between 1937 and 1939. Bataille's interests in myth and ritual replaced the priority he had given to social action. He began to explore mysticism, but not a Christian one in the sense that John of the Cross or Teresa of Avila longed for unity with God. Instead, "I prefer using the word 'atheological' to describe the entry into the sacred and the gods, as well as the principle of sovereignty, the negation of a perfect God who has the attributes of a thing and of reason" (OC, VIII, 394 f.). Bataille's mystical visions transcended the chaos and solitude he experienced in life. The practice of yoga helped him to focus on a sense of inner peace and intellectual tranquility derived from Zen Buddhism. Nevertheless, he was never freed from his anguish and suffering. His own internal struggles were bound up in the etymology of sacred, coming from the word *sacer,* which means both defiled and holy. This opposition plays a part in the thesis he later developed in *L'Erotisme* that the bond between transgression and taboo is innate. Cast-off objects, such as cadavers, become sacred for Bataille. His necrophilia, especially evident in the last part of *Le Bleu du ciel,* is part of the base materialism that his mysticism encompassed during his experiments with it during the 1940s.

Although Bataille was not a member of the military during World War II, the war was ever-present to him. Certain pages of his essays *Sur Nietzsche* (1945) reflect his anxiety as a civilian victim of the military bombings carried out by both the Allies and the Nazis. Of course, he had experienced war before, as a member of the military and as a civilian escaping the siege of Reims with his mother. Just as he produced a pious reflection, "Notre Dame de Rheims," during the siege of Reims, so did World War II become for him "a means of agonized reflection" and "a nostalgia for ecstatic states (OC, V, 540). Whereas during the creation of "Notre Dame de Rheims" his father's life was in the balance, this time Laure's and Heine's lives became the stakes for his reflections. His biography of Laure was appended to his and Leiris's edition of her collected works. In the process of writing about her, Bataille was upset by "the anguish of justifying life" (OC, VI, 276). And so he embarked upon his inner experiment.[30] Bataille's friendship with Blanchot was especially crucial during the war. Blanchot's fascination with presence and nonpresence, already a phenomenological topic (especially for Husserl and Heidegger), combined with Bataille's attraction to the Socratic problems of self-knowledge and nonknowledge to become the core of his mystical reflections.

In the apartment of Denise Rollin in the fall of 1941, Bataille initiated what he called *le Collège Socratique* (the Socratic College). This seminar evolved from the debates and discussions Bataille sponsored during the war years. These involved two basic groups: the first consisted of Queneau, Leiris, and Michel Fardoulis-Lagrange; the second assembled Pierre Prévost, Louis Ollivier, Romain Petitot, and Xavier de Lignac. Blanchot and Bataille participated in both. With these groups, Bataille began to develop some of the interests discussed by Socrates, namely the nature of self-knowledge and nonknowledge (**le non-savoir**).[31]

In 1941, Bataille published *Madame Edwarda* under the pseudonym Pierre Angélique. This pseudonym combines Bataille's interests in base materialism (*pierre* means stone) and mysticism (*angélique* means angelic). The communication between the two is at times found for him in pornography, where the two extremes of the human condition are united. As he claims, "I only wanted to describe in *Edwarda* a movement of independent ecstasy, if not from the depression of a life of debauchery, at least from the so-called sexual trauma" (OC, III, 493). Bataille would continue to reiterate the links between the two extremes in various guises throughout his writings.

Bataille sold one copy of his pornographic text *Le Mort* to a bookstore in 1944.[32] This text, as well as probably his most outrageous pornographic text, *Ma Mère*, was not generally available until after his death. His abiding interest in pornography during the war years is worth noting, since anguish about the Occupation, the presence of base materialism in the reporting of wartime violence, and his own problems with tuberculosis haunted him during this period.

The war inspired him to write about his own variation of mysticism in *L'Expérience intérieure*. His own experiences of bonding with men in the military returned as he wrote about a "mystical army" organized around the same ideological causes: "In order to fix a correct and formal reality for this common fervor, it groups its soldiers around a sacred emblem in much the same way that a church organizes the houses which form a village" (OC, II, 236). The geographical setting of French villages grounded Bataille's mystical experiments with ideological armies into a vivid image of the unity that the bonding of an army can achieve.

The theme of communication, which marks his pornographic writing, was also essential for the *Collège Socratique*. In this *Collège* Bataille defined what communication meant for him: "Communicating means trying to achieve unity and being one for many, which the word 'communion' has succeeded in meaning" (OC, VI, 279). Thus, the concept of communion, which was crucial for the religious rituals of Catholicism and had been realized practically in Bataille's work with groups throughout the 1920s and 1930s, surfaced as a concept worthy of elaborating within Bataille's discussion groups. During these years, Bataille was working on poems for his *L'Archangélique* (note the theme of transcendence even beyond the "angelic" identity of his *Madame Edwarda*), the abstract propositions for his own version of mysticism in *L'Expérience intérieure* (1943), his philosophical propositions for *Sur Nietzsche* (1945), and his economic reflections for *La Part maudite* (1949). He designed a master work called *Somme athéologique* with three volumes: *L'Expérience intérieure*, *Le Coupable* (1944), and *Sur Nietzsche*. These volumes constitute Bataille's major philosophical work. I discuss them in more detail in chapter 3.

Bataille's struggle with pulmonary tuberculosis became so severe in 1942 that he had to retire from his position at the Bibliothèque Nationale in Paris to convalesce in Vézelay, Burgundy. There, he exchanged mistresses, replacing Diane Rollin with Diane Kotchoubey de Beauharnais. During this period, Bataille began his long association with Jacques Lacan, who had married Sylvia, the first Mrs. Bataille. He also met Romain Rolland, his neighbor in Vézelay. These personal encounters contributed to Bataille's very productive intellectual period.

Leiris introduced Bataille to Sartre, who had written a devastating reply to *L'Expérience intérieure*. Although Bataille used the vocabulary of Christian mystical theology,[33] he wanted to create a mysticism that was not transcendent. However, Sartre accused Bataille of idealism. Bataille took Sartre seriously, published a response to Sartre, and actually modified his intellectual stance. (I present their arguments in chapter 4.) Sartre, curiously, would never review another of Bataille's works, whereas Bataille continued to respond to Sartre's books. Nevertheless, the two men developed mutual respect for each other's writings. During 1944, Bataille and Sartre often met to discuss their intellectual positions.

Meanwhile, Bataille fell in love with Diane Kotchoubey, and he began writing the poems for *L'Alleluiah*, which has been called the catechism of his atheology (Surya, 432). Bataille was thus very active during the war years despite his convalescence. In October 1944, he returned to Paris to live in a new apartment, his 10th residence since the beginning of the war.

The surrealists also reacted to *L'Expérience intérieure*, with the 1943 publication of *Nom de Dieu* as a response to Bataille's apparently overly abstract reflections. Michael Richardson notes that Fardoulis-Lagrange helped to draw Bataille closer to surrealism after the war (Richardson, *Absence,* 3). During the 1940s, however, Bataille was still alienated from the surrealists, among whom he had created dissension in their separation from Breton. Bataille remarks in an interview with Madeleine Chapsal that "surrealism appears to me . . . a rage against life itself.[34]" Of course, Bataille implies that his own work was an affirmation of the vitality denied by the surrealist ventures. Bataille's vitality during the war years was once again found in his struggles. He and Maurice Blanchot became good friends during this period. Blanchot records that in 1940 Bataille expressed regret for his article "La Structure psychologique du fascisme," published in *La Critique sociale* in 1933–1934, because of its apparent flirtation with fascism as Bataille expressed his horror at Nazism. Though Bataille was fond of saying "I am war incarnate" (OC, I, 557), he was increasingly disenchanted with politics and yearned for a return to his mystical religion. Bataille's understanding of religion is akin to that of Hermann Cohen—that religion is the desire for the undesirable. Bataille adds his own engagement of that desire with myth, magic, shamans, and the sacred: all of which are brought together in Jules Monnerot's *La Poésie moderne et le sacré*, published in 1945. This book had a considerable influence on Bataille, who had been experimenting with poetry, had played the role of a shaman, and was intrigued by such priestly metamorphoses[35] as well as by the magical role of the sacred in melding people together for a common cause. These interests also guided Bataille back to surrealism (e.g., Monnerot's reflection that "the dream is a guarantee of myth"[36]), with which he collaborated once again in 1947.

As the war ended, Bataille returned to Paris. There he realized a dream he had discussed with Blanchot and others during the war: the founding of a journal that could serve as an international forum for debate about books, based on the premise that the political problems of nationalism should not preclude intellectual inquiry. Certainly, Bataille had extraordinary language skills and had read deeply across cultures. He possessed writing and reading skills in English, Spanish, German, and Italian. He read Greek and Latin and had studied Russian and Tibetan. He brought these talents to bear as he, Blanchot, and others founded the journal *Critique* in 1946. This journal also extended Blanchot's influence significantly by publishing his insights into the most challenging texts from New Criticism, Structuralism, and poststructuralism at least until 1970.[37]

## 1946–1962: Eroticism and Death as Literary Problems

With the advent of *Critique*, Bataille became a literary shaman as he advocated the reading of books that made an intellectual difference. In fact, he sometimes modified his own stances through these exchanges.[38] Rather than struggle with the incompatibilities of being a writer, with its attendant responsibilities to be engaged and to lead the masses, especially as defined by Julian Benda and then Sartre after the war, Bataille claimed that "I simply chose to *live*" (OC, XII, 17). However, his "living" was much more complicated than a simple existence. He became involved politically once again. He openly supported the Marshall Plan in 1947, edited a special issue of the journal *Actualité* on a free Spain, and wrote the piece "L'Absence de Mythe" for the catalogue of the 1947 surrealist exhibition on myth. He was making political statements as a writer.

In his private life, his daughter Julie was born to Diane de Beauharnais in 1948. He married Diane in 1951. Out of his struggles with his tuberculosis and the deaths of his close friends during the war, he found a vitality intimately linked with those experiences. Although *Erotisme* was not published until 1957, some of his reflections were produced during the late 1940s. His proximity to his own death and the eroticism of his new life with Diane echoed in his writings: "Eroticism opens one to death; death opens up the negation of individual duration" (OC, X, 29). He struggled with his writing and was upset when his longtime associate, Jules Monnerot, revealed to the press Bataille's authorship of the pornographic stories *Madame Edwarda* (1941) and *L'Histoire de l'oeil* (1928), both originally published under pseudonyms. Bataille's displeasure is noteworthy. He was still trying to obtain employment and was concerned that his reputation as a pornographic writer would discourage his appointment to the post of librarian. His use of a mask for his name was quite widespread already. In 1924, he claimed to have used "Troppmann" (a name recovered in *Le Bleu du ciel*) for "W.C.," a work he later destroyed. In 1934, he also used "Louis Trente" to disguise his identity as the author of the essay "Le Petit." In 1947, he used "Dianus" and the narrator Monsieur Alpha for "L'Alleluiah—Le Catéchisme de Dianus," "Histoire des rats," and *Le Coupable*. Bataille explained that the pseudonym Dianus, a name from Roman mythology, reunites "the appeal of a bearded woman and a dying god with blood trickling down his throat" (OC, V, 437). Thus, at least in this case and probably with his other masks also, Bataille experimented with being what he was not—a woman and a dying god. For Monnerot, the author of *La Poésie moderne et le sacré,* which was influential to Bataille's subsequent work, to expose the masquerade was also to make Bataille's art vulnerable to exposure of the mystery of his religious ritual. Bataille never used another pseudonym after Monnerot's revelation. In the late 1940s, Bataille wrote, appropriately: "I believe that the sacred is dead from the excessive elevation of the spirit which was brought about by an uncontrollable fear about what is fascinating and violent" (OC, XI, 568, n. 1). His fear had to do with being out of control, perhaps of his destiny but also about the interpretation of his writing.

In 1949, Bataille obtained a position as librarian in Charpentras. It was not Paris, where he was more widely known for his philandering and authoring of erotic texts. Nevertheless, he was once more gainfully employed, and he and Diane settled down to a provincial life. In 1951 he moved to the city of Orléans where he was placed in charge of the municipal library. Despite these positions of employment, Bataille was in constant financial difficulty until his death in 1962, when his friends admitted that they had to rescue him from debt several times.[39] Appropriately, Bataille published his major work on economic theory (*La Part maudite*) in 1949. This book develops his theories on expense, rather than surplus, being the major ingredient missing from modern economics.

Bataille did not give up his fascination with religion and the sacred. In fact, he reworked his short story "Eponine," published in 1949, into his first published novel, *L'Abbé C.,* published in 1950. The title, with its pun on the apparent simplicity of the alphabet, points toward his obsession with the priestly role. However, Bataille herein complicates religion with an eroticism that for him has been coldly marginalized by institutionalized rituals.[40] In his novel, Bataille places the cleric at the center of rituals that dramatize the stakes of human eroticism with its anguish, frustration, and mystical return to the unity of being. This unity of being revolves around the issue of male power, namely the virility/impotence (**la virilité, l'impuissance**) of the priest. As I have mentioned, the question of impotence haunted Bataille since his childhood experience with his father's syphilis. The words impotence and power (**pouvoir**) are found throughout his work, as is typical of male authors who wrote and survived the 1930s and emerged with an ethic linking virility and "action." This concern often inspires dismay in feminist critics, such as Susan Rubin Suleiman.[41] Nevertheless, in his writings Bataille struggles with his own sexuality and its links with the rest of humanity. In "Eponine," the title of which is also the name of the story's female heroine, the narrator delineates the problem: "What attracts me in a priest is certainly what he doesn't have."[40] The priest's sexual life is then elaborated in subtle ways within *L'Abbé C.* through the mirror of his twin brother. Eponine must laugh at the sight of the priest who is an object of her sexual fantasy and yet performs these abstract rituals as if he were inhuman and godlike. Although the novel did not attract the attention from Parisian critics that it deserved, it grounds Bataille's mystical views of sex, the sacred, and ritual in a tale of haunting Gothic images, such as a climb inside a church tower whose dungeonlike depth is described as the empty abyss of anguish that threatens to engulf the narrator, the other characters, and even Bataille himself. This image foreshadows Bataille's admission at a conference in 1954 in Geneva that "I take pleasure, at least sometimes, in anguish. . . . I mean that I drown myself, I abandon myself in it completely" (Laure, 286).

Given Bataille's fascination with the abyss of anguish, it is no surprise that he explored the prehistoric art found in the Lascaux caves. His book about this art and another explaining the paintings of Edouard Manet were published by Skira in 1955 and gave him a reputation for art criticism. The English translations of these works were soon brought to Great Britain and to the United States, where they enjoyed some celebrity. On the one hand, Bataille sought to present "the types of elation" (Chapsal, 233) expressed by the artist(s) of Lascaux. Bataille discovered and elaborated on an erotic mysticism for what appear to be naive, heterogeneous drawings of early cave dwellers. He developed his vision of the origin of human art with the breadth he inherited from Heidegger[43] and others, as will be discussed in chapter 2. On the other hand, Bataille's book on Manet proposed that artist's tableaux as continuations of what Goya began, that is, the destruction of academic painting in favor of the positioning of death, terror, and the anguish accompanying them (OC, IX, 31). According to Surya, André Malraux and Bataille influenced each other here and influenced as well the evolution of the history of art (Surya, 572 ff.).

Meanwhile, 1955 also brought ill health to Bataille. He never fully recovered and spent the rest of his years, until 1962, literally struggling with his own death. From time to time, he was able to reach out and speak on issues. In 1957, he gave an interview to Marguerite Duras, published in *France Observateur*. He was a celebrity because in that year alone, four of his works were published: *Le Bleu du ciel* (written in 1935), *La Littérature et le mal*, *L'Erotisme*, and the third edition of *Madame Edwarda*, this time with his own introduction. In the interview with Duras, Bataille noted the importance of the comic in his vision: "We cannot seriously reflect upon God without being struck by a sense of the comic so profound that we would be excused for not recognizing it as comic."[44] His curious smile in the face of this comedy, as exhibited in the photograph on the frontispiece of this book, helped to relieve him, for however brief a moment, from the extreme stress of his anguish, his impending death, and his isolation from the life of Paris. Bataille returned to Paris in 1961 to give testimony at the trial of publisher Jean-Jacques Pauvert, whom the state sued to prevent the publication of the Marquis de Sade's work on the grounds that it was pornography. Bataille testified to the literary value of Sade.

Eroticism and words became even more crucial to Bataille in a Godless life. Pierre Klossowski bears witness to these values: "If there is no God who created the flesh, there is no longer anything for the spirit except the excesses of language to reduce the excesses of the flesh to silence; there is then nothing more 'verbal' than the excesses of the flesh."[45] And Bataille managed, despite his illness, to work on his erotic masterpiece, *Ma Mère*, which was published posthumously. Once again, it was written under a pseudonym, this time that of Pierre Angélique. Maryline Lukacher remarks that Thomas Aquinas was known as Père Angélique, "the angelic father" (Lukacher, 165). In *Ma Mère*, Pierre says, almost in an echo of Bataille: "About religion, which I had believed at first to bother me profoundly from the depths of my being, I now ceased to even think about it."[46] There is much to be said about Bataille's substitution for Thomistic theology, in this case, an atheology in which eroticism and the mother's body[47] are developed as components of the son's blindness to himself. In *La Mère*, masks are crucial images separating the mother from her son. Likewise, Bataille lived his life disguised, while his creative writings allowed him to expose the masks of guilt, anxiety, desire, frustration, joy, mysticism, and loneliness. As Surya well observes, Bataille died at the age of 65 without ever taking off his masks (Surya, 117). And yet the narrative "I" of his writings remains as

## *Chapter Two*

# Inclinations

Bataille's extensive readings modified the course of his vision for atheology. Other writers provided him with the major questions that generated the anxiety with which he struggled. Rather than calling these writers influences upon Bataille, I choose to call them inclinations because, although they provided tendencies and directions, Bataille did not so much adopt their tendencies as adapt them to his own vision. These inclinations were presented in chapter 1 and can also be found in the chronology section at the beginning of this book. The word chronology is somewhat misleading regarding how these writers affected Bataille. He revisited them throughout his writings in a manner imitative of Giambatista Vico's spiraling history in his *New Science* of 1744. As Bataille's vision evolved, he continually adapted the visions of these writers as if from the perspective of a spire, that is, at different points in his intellectual evolution. My presentation considers the intellectual content of these inclinations for Bataille and how they coalesced, through his modification and adaptation to atheology, to comprise his own unique vision. Let us review the major sources for these inclinations.

Bataille's exposure to the Marquis de Sade is the significant point of orientation in the grounding of Bataille's early, pious concerns with religion. Some critics of Bataille, such as Daniel Hawley, go so far as to call Bataille "the twentieth century Sade."[1] Certainly, Bataille reiterates and recasts Sade's concerns with death, sovereignty, and community to provide a more expansive view of the "complete human being" (**l'homme entier;** OC, VI, 20) than even Sade was capable of formulating. Although Sade provides Bataille with the basic paradigm for a complete human being by integrating base materialism with a frank attitude toward eroticism, Bataille adapts this principle to the ideal of action made so prevalent from the 1920s to the 1950s by Julien Benda, André Malraux, Drieu la Rochelle, and Jean-Paul Sartre. However, Bataille does much more than transform Sade with a view toward political action; by standing on the shoulders of other intellectual giants, he projects Sade's insights farther than could be seen in the eighteenth century.

Bataille found, in reading Friedrich Nietzsche, inclinations that push Sade beyond the visions of Sadean writing. Leon Chestov guided Bataille's reading of Nietzsche and provided an existential view from the Russian experiences of Dostoyevsky and Tolstoy. This led Bataille to modify Sade's principle of sovereignty (**la souveraineté**) and the ideal of the complete human being. From Nietzsche, Bataille learns the inclinations of resentment, laughter, and an orientation toward heterogeneity (**l'hétérogénéité**) that he finds indispensable in developing his atheological attitude.

Alexander Kojève, with whom Bataille studied in the 1930s, provided Bataille with a necessary orientation toward Hegel.[2] For Bataille, Hegel is the sage who defines wisdom as the crucial principle of sovereignty. The master/slave dialectic in Hegel inclines Bataille toward the negative in its orientation of the slave's need to rebel. These insights guide Bataille into his vision of the crucial attitudes toward "absolute dismemberment," the satisfaction of death, and the end of history.

Community is also an abiding concern of Bataille throughout his work. Emile Durkheim, who proposes that social structures prevail upon the behavior of individuals, guides Bataille's inclinations toward the nature of the social, the links between the social and the sacred, and the social need for myth. Although his solutions are not satisfactory in their scientific pretensions, Durkheim does outline some key issues with which Bataille struggles regarding the role of community.

Community for Bataille is developed through communication and communion. His friend Alfred Métraux guides Bataille in learning about exchange as a system of noneconomic communication as elaborated in Marcel Mauss's theories of potlatch (**le potlatch**). Mauss orients Bataille toward yet another inclination about the relationships among the sacred, society, and a theory of communication. This recognition of the process of social exchange through customs such as gift giving helps Bataille to elaborate a theory of mysticism that brings together elements of the sacred, myth, and anthropological insights into community.

The glue that holds the community together was intriguing for Bataille. Reading Karl Marx introduced Bataille to the importance of economics within the framework of dialectical materialism. Marx's communism attracted Bataille during the early 1930s when Bataille was associated with Boris Souvarine, the anti-Stalinist communist and director of the *Cercle Communiste Démocratique*. The inclinations provided by Marx were not only in the sphere of political activity but also in Bataille's positioning of class struggle and the role of religion within society.

Max Weber's insights into Calvinism and capitalism allow Bataille to elaborate his own theory of economic exchange as another factor in social structuring. The Calvinist and capitalist juncture in Weber's model provides Bataille with the "straw man" against which Bataille posits his own economic theory of expenditure. Weber's development of the principles of surplus and accumulation advocated by both Calvinism and capitalism sets up a systematic worldview whose totalism (**la totalisation**) is undermined by Bataille's evolving views of transgression, sacrifice, and expenditure as guiding principles for a world economy capable of generosity (**la générosité**) and the recognition of pluralistic communities.

Finally, I retrace the attractiveness of Miguel de Unamuno and Blaise Pascal to Bataille's atheological tendencies. Although both writers were Christian believers, their theories about living on the edge of belief and nonbelief in God have echoes in Bataille's own anxiety about being on the edge of the abyss of nothingness. Unamuno's concerns with suffering, skepticism, impotence, the acknowledgment of impossibility, the attractiveness of Tibetan mysticism, and the social and economic factors in the sacred all find elaborations in Bataille's writings. Bataille's negative stance toward Pascal's wager about the existence of God also calls upon Pascal's penchant for blending science with reflections about the sacred.

All of these inclinations that affected Bataille help us to recognize how he differs from his predecessors and what he has contributed to philosophy, economics, sociology, and the history of ideas through his writings. Let us examine in closer detail where these inclinations began and where Bataille took them.

## Sade: Sovereignty and Imprisonment

Although the Marquis de Sade's writings are marked by his eroticism and the violence associated with it, Bataille did learn about the universal nature of these experiences from Sade. In the eighteenth century, Sade wrote most of his Gothic novels during his imprisonment in the Bastille and his close brush with the guillotine. His writings, therefore, exemplify a model of the eroticism of sex in the face of an uncontrollable fate and impending death. This model is based on narratives of erotic experiences that demonstrate controlled desire, a rational sense of pleasure in the face of death, and the accompanying anguish of waiting for and expecting one's own death. Bataille found Sade's recognition of a situation to be universally common to all humanity. In 1956, for the pornography trial of Jean-Jacques Pauvert, who published Sade's complete works, Bataille gave a deposition stating that ". . . what was innovative in the Marquis de Sade . . . is the recognition that humanity found satisfaction in the contemplation of death and suffering" (OC, XII, 453). This satisfaction comes with the sovereign attitude that then governs desire, community, and a human sense of the sacred. From Sade, Bataille learned that sovereign attitudes are those that are "gratuitous, without utility, only serving for what they are, never subordinated to subsequent results" (OC, X, 184).

Sade's atheism in the face of the absurdity of death led him to develop the sovereignty that Bataille adapts. Bataille takes Sade's insights into eroticism one step further, that is, from a personal to a community-oriented yearning. The denial of God, in accepting death and the anxious reality that comes with such an acceptance, is accompanied by a profound affirmation identified by Bataille as "that of a dangerous sovereignty of violence, (which) tended at least to maintain an anguish which brought to consciousness a nostalgia for intimacy, on the level of which only violence has the force to elevate us" (OC, VII, 307).

Violence is indeed "a dangerous sovereignty" because it is expressed on the brink of individual anxiety. The danger is both to the individual and to the hoped-for community (coming from "a nostalgia for intimacy"). The individual, for both Sade and Bataille, is predominately a majority-group male ("Sade's sovereign male . . . is free in front of the others and is no less a victim of his own sovereignty" [OC, X, 174]). Sade's narrators are usually male, and the victims of their violence are female. The "danger" is in keeping it that way, thus isolating men from women. The memory of community is projected forward to a future that may very well not exist, since the subject is threatened by impending death. Bataille thus puts Sade at center stage for the implications of Sadean writing for community, which Bataille sought intellectually, emotionally, and politically throughout his life. Of course, we should heed Michael Richardson's proviso that community also threatens the individual with "this sense of undifferentiation, this collapse into otherness, [which] is what Sade both fears and denies" (Richardson, *Absence,* 16).

Sade thus enables Bataille to portray the personal struggle between the spirit and the flesh in the "complete human being." This is what pornography expresses for both Sade and Bataille (Klossowski, 126). This struggle simultaneously explodes and implodes in Sade, according to Bataille: "There was in his agitation the equivalent of an explosion which tore him apart, but which nevertheless suffocated him" (OC, X, 618). Sade received considerable public approbation for those erotic works published during his lifetime. By contrast, Bataille's own pornographic writings were private ventures as he insisted upon their anonymity during his lifetime. Perhaps he feared the public outcry against his public service career. Susan Sontag claims that "because Bataille possessed a finer and more profound sense of transgression . . . what he describes seems somehow more potent and outrageous than the most lurid orgies staged by Sade."[3] Bataille did, however, testify for the right of Pauvert to publish the complete works of Sade in the public trial in 1956 when Bataille was already beset by serious and ultimately terminal illness.

In the final analysis, Sade must be seen as a point of reference for Bataille. Whereas in 1930 André Breton argued that Bataille's writing was not in the same league as that of Sade,[4] Daniel Hawley now claims that Bataille is the twentieth-century Sade, as I just mentioned. This battle between Sade and Bataille is so reductionist as to ignore either one's virtuosity. It is far better to hear Sade as one of the voices adapted by Bataille and to agree with Richardson that "to see Bataille's thought through Sade or vice versa, is fundamentally to misunderstand it" (Richardson, *Absence,* 15). Let us now see how Nietzsche contributed to Bataille's modification of the principles of sovereignty and the complete human being.

## Nietzsche: Chestov and the Death of God

Bataille admired how Nietzsche thought. In 1923, when Bataille began a poetic reading of Nietzsche, he was still influenced by the theological reflections of his seminary education, which was Hegelian and idealistic in spirit. The philosopher Leon Chestov, who had left Russia and its Revolution in 1920, invited Bataille to join a group of students that met nights in his apartment in Paris. From 1922 to 1925 he influenced Bataille by introducing him to readings of Nietzsche and Dostoyevsky. The anti-idealistic and anti-Hegelian postures of Chestov guided Bataille's readings of both writers. These readings conformed to Bataille's less pious inclinations than he exhibited in *Notre Dame de Rheims*, for example, as he searched for alternatives to the Catholic theological system.

Bataille heard Chestov trace Nietzsche's own intellectual journey away from Christian morality toward the alternate abysses of the Nietzschean ultimatum "know or die."[5] Knowledge offered the promise of expanding the narrow piety of institutionalized theology. Knowledge itself was an abyss for Bataille as he viewed nonknowledge to be a continuation of the commitment toward human epistemology. He observed that God "as an effect of nonknowledge is knowable as is laughter and the sacred" (OC, VIII, 229). This insight is linked to Dostoyevsky's denial of his previous faith as if it were mud covering up existence. Bataille continues by saying that "God is, in effect, the indifference to the false possibility of going further" (OC, X, 674). Chestov, in combination with Maurice Heine, guided Bataille to a reading of Nietzsche that reinforced Dostoyevsky's existential position in the face of death, the death of God and humanity. Reflecting upon the *Acéphale*'s atheological orientation, Pierre Klossowski looks back upon Chestov's influence on Bataille[6] to underscore that the Russian authors looked upon Christ's death, since it is often reiterated in the practices of Christianity, as the event reinforcing the death of God not as a simple atheism but as a continuing activity. In other words, Nietzsche's call for knowledge as an alternative to death was seen as an ongoing challenge.

Although Bataille continually refers to Nietzsche in his writings, he does not speak so much about Nietzsche as he does about how he has assimilated Nietzsche's thought for his own purposes. His *Sur Nietzsche*, for example, gives very little of a developed reading of Nietzsche. It is the spirit of Nietzsche that lives in Bataille. For example, in *Le Bleu du ciel*, the name of Nietzsche is not cited as such. But the following passage is admirably Nietzschean in its portrayal of the "herd instinct": "Men are valets . . . if there is one who gives the impression of being a master, there are others who are exploding from the desire to be one . . . but those who bow before nothing are in prisons and underground . . . and prison or death for these . . . means servitude for all the others . . ." (OC, III, 428). Of course, Dostoyevsky's *Notes from the Underground* is also implied in this portrayal of the Nietzschean herd instinct.

Bataille is sensitive to the misappropriation of Nietzsche. He especially disputes the Nazi mainstream's claims for Nietzsche as its philosophical precedent with such concepts as superman, Aryan, and racial purity. Bataille argues that Nietzsche claimed to be racially Polish, using arguments about the Slavic etymology of his name (OC, XI, 10). As a rebuttal to fascism's acquisition of Nietzsche as its own, Bataille announced in *Combat* that his book *Nietzsche et le communisme* would appear in May 1946 (OC, XI, 557, n. 1). Although the book was never published, Bataille did argue against the right-wing ideological readings of Nietzsche.

In his rebuttal, Bataille promoted the importance of the principle of sovereignty as Nietzschean in spirit. This sovereignty operates on the level of morality, as Jean-Louis Baudry indicates.[7] The Church in France has a historical link with sovereignty, placing sovereign lords above the people and endowing aristocracy with the prestige of moral sanction (OC, XII, 26). The basic principle advocated by the Church in politics is that human sovereignty is negated before the "personal sovereignty" of a transcendent being (OC, XII, 527), in other words, God. Bataille then inverts this relationship and speaks of "negative" or mystical theology (OC, VIII, 29) that leads to atheology and the sovereignty of humanity refusing to be submissive.

Nietzsche provides Bataille with the parameters to modify Sade's presentation of sovereignty with insights into the importance of community and communion. Bataille's interpretation of Nietzsche does change over time. As Allen Weiss develops, Bataille continues to advocate the communion of sovereign individuals even though the nature of that communion evolves from his political involvements with the proletariat in the 1930s, to the intellectual collegiality leading up to the *Collège de Sociologie,* to the secret projects of the *Acéphale,* and finally to the mystical associations of his atheological visions.[8] With Nietzsche, Bataille seeks an alternative to Christianity with its "negation of human sovereignty in favor of a transcendent sovereignty based on individual sovereignty" (OC, XII, 527). In pursuing an almost anti-Christian attitude, Bataille finds camaraderie in Albert Camus's reading of Nietzsche and affirms a similar position by defining sovereignty as "the fact of not being compliant" (OC, XII, 163).

There is also the community with others who are not compliant. The expression of this rejection of compliance has a positive, bonding effect for Bataille by creating an alternative "holy communion." This communion is sacred and Nietzschean in its creation of an energy often marginalized by mainstream "moral" thinking. Annette Michelson portrays Bataille's reflections well in this regard: "Thus, death and decay in their diverse aspects and figures, the body's excreta (tears, sweat, shit, blood, and menstrual blood), those substances cast off, excluded, hedged around with silence and interdiction, partake of the sacred. And, manifestly, as well, those states of loss of self we know in rage, laughter, orgy, and sacrifice. We may say of such states, as Bataille does indeed say, that these are states of sovereignty."[9]

Such a base materialism is a consequence of acknowledging the death of God expounded by Nietzsche while also focusing upon the complete human being as conceived by Nietzsche and developed by Bataille. Indeed, for Bataille, "the death of God posits the problem of human sovereignty on a spiritual plane" (OC, VI, 251). Rather than looking toward transcendence to be saved, the complete person renounces any form of external domination, whether through the God of organized religion or the various hierarchies that feudalism and capitalism hoisted into position to oversee human activity. Bataille thus conceptualizes human sovereignty as a way to acknowledge control and responsibility for the self. In contrast with the "herd instinct" that Nietzsche observes in much human activity, human sovereignty can also be expressed with others in a community of action.

Action has a distinct meaning for Bataille. Following upon Nietzsche's turning away from the herd, Bataille carefully refuses the social validation of action or engagement popularized during the 1920s through the 1940s by Julien Benda, André Malraux, and Jean-Paul Sartre. Instead, Bataille points to the problems of the validation of action by others (see chapter 4 for the debate between Bataille and Sartre). Bataille would have the whole human being recognize the traps therein: "When the whole person recognizes that one's irrational being is exterior to action and when it is recognized that there is a trap and a loss of one's totality in every possible manifestation of transcendence, we renounce the irrational hierarchies (feudal and capitalist) in the domain of activity" (OC, VI, 24 n.).

In the place of feudal and capitalist hierarchies, human sovereignty values authenticity as the prime mover of action (OC, XII, 26). In medieval times the Church encouraged sovereignty in monarchies and the military with their need for discipline and hierarchy (OC, I, 357). Although Bataille recognizes that the Church is rejected in this regard by Nietzsche, as well as by Gide and Camus under Nietzsche's influence, Bataille likewise does learn from Christianity to place revolt at center stage (OC, X, 682). However authentic the revolt may be, Bataille believes that his life and his writings are a communal experience with Nietzsche (OC, VI, 33), just as the whole human being is continually drawn toward community ("The desire for community constantly agitated such a person," OC, VI, 32). In his *L'Abbé C.*, with its title that refers to the alphabet and thus a primer in terms of establishing human sovereignty, the character Eponine, who is helping the priest to understand his own eroticism, is repelled by the mystical attitude of his ecclesiastical rituals. Her attitude is described as "resentment."[10] This mirrors Bataille's resentment about his early pious Catholic education. The word resentment is favored by Nietzsche to describe what Camus later embodies for Bataille: ". . . nothing is stronger in us than rebellion" (OC, XII, 195). Such a view of rebellion is the essence of human activity for Bataille.

Despite Nietzsche's serious commitment to the psychology of human action in rebellion, he also teaches, especially in *Ecce Homo*, the crucial role of laughter. This is a positive life force, sometimes identified by Bataille as the energy of the sun. Bataille adapts from Nietzsche the modeling of expense and excess on the sun, which cannot hold back its light and heat.[11] The sun is the model for Nietzsche's *Übermensch* and becomes for Bataille a model of economics as well as for the human giving of energy that cannot be contained. Bataille listens to Nietzsche and incorporates the laughter and tears of Dionysus in mystical reflections on sovereignty. For Bataille, laughter and tears are spontaneous expressions of the body's vital interests; they participate in the inner experiment of nonknowledge whereby the body communicates meaningless elimination. Regarding laughter, Bataille, unlike Nietzsche, who has a sense of humor about himself, warrants Sartre's observation that "he tells us that he laughs, but he does not make us laugh."[12] Bataille takes his writing about laughter seriously as a component of his heterogeneous vision, that is, as an alternative to totalizing ideologies or hierarchical systems in which the individual's sovereignty is subordinated to a "greater" good.

The stakes of appropriating Nietzsche's thought are serious, especially concerning racism and sexism. If sexism can be seen as a form of racism, as I maintain that it is, then Bataille's defense of Nietzsche's racism is ennobling because of Bataille's own flirtation with fascism and "virile" attitudes. Although Bataille could not see his own sexism or Nietzsche's misogyny, he did reject the Nazi recuperation of Nietzsche for its racist propaganda. At one point, Bataille even accused the moral philosopher Emmanuel Lévinas of not bothering to justify his identification of Nietzsche with "a racist attitude" (OC, I, 462). Instead of reducing Nietzsche to selectively racist portions of his work, Bataille recommends reading all of Nietzsche and seeing therein "the eternal return" of the Nietzschean "ecstatic vision" (OC, I, 510).

The intersection of Nietzsche and Bataille must also be tempered by Bataille's reading of Hegel. Although Bataille began reading Hegel relatively late (between 1933 and 1939) compared to his reading of Nietzsche (begun in 1923), Bataille adapted another inclination from the lectures on Hegel given by Alexandre Kojève. As Jean-Michel Besnier comments, "Kojève revealed that Hegel was right—that history had ended."[13] So the death of God had also to be matched with the death of history as it was known until Hegel.

## Hegel: Kojève and the Master/Slave Dialectic

For Hegel, the end of history is accomplished by the development of human freedom as a rational process through which the dialectic takes place. Alexander Kojève lectured at the *École Pratique des Hautes Études* on the writings of the youthful Hegel, who presents the slave as the model for the working of the dialectic of human freedom. The principled slave is Hegel's projection of humanity in search of its sovereignty from the master. Bataille then sees social rebellion as a Hegelian search for the escape from the determination of history, that is, from the masters who are responsible for human slavery. In contrast with Friedrich Engels, who, Bataille says, in 1885 stopped believing in the principle of the negation of a negation, Hegel offers the wisdom that the dialectic of history is an internal human process by which individuals must differ internally in order to negate the impending negation of death. The master/slave dialectic thus operates within the rational process of human freedom. While for Bataille "class struggle becomes . . . the most grandiose form of social expenditure . . . which threatens the very existence of the masters" (OC, I, 316), this view empowers the negative principle of the dialectic, the subversive tendency of human freedom to resist being totalized by forces in history. Instead of the human subject determined in history, the individual who refuses to be subjugated in that refusal seeks personal sovereignty and thus makes history.

The master, in this context, is distinguished from Bataille's sovereign.[14] The master is more than the sovereign king in the feudal hierarchy or the sovereign capital of capitalist systems. The master appears in various forms of domination to restrict human freedom and thereby engages the dialectical opposition to what Hegel maintains is the natural progression of human independence from lesser to greater freedom. In his 1930 study of fascism (OC, I, 339–71), Bataille notes that the chief political problem is neither fascism nor antifascism but the state itself, that is, government that tries to regulate human activity.

The resolution of the problem is in the work of the slave who masters the material quality of life by embracing the work that conditions the slavery (OC, I, 433). Work brings recognition to the worker of the material conditions of oppression and of the necessity to break the bonds that lead to oppression. Thus the revolt of the slave is born out of the vision provided by Bataille that "the essential . . . [is] work and play" (OC, X, 682). The playfulness of the slave's condition is realized through rebellion against the master.

The slave becomes the incarnation of the principle of negation against negation and the reason for being of the master. For Bataille, the slave is the most interesting feature of Hegel's dialectic because "subversion alone gives culture the sense of humanity's agreement with itself" (OC, XII, 449). The rebellion by the slave challenges the authority of the master and creates contestation for the one who rules by playing on the anguish of death in the slave. Typical of such a master for Bataille is the assertive military leader who is "the incarnation of this violent negation" (OC, I, 358) by the master insistent upon dominating the slave. The slave then has the power of confronting the master and rebelling against the asserted domination, thus affirming the negation of negation within the base materialism of Hegel's doctrine, which, for Bataille, is "an extraordinary and very perfect system of reduction" (OC, I, 221). Reduction is meant positively here in that Hegel makes one aware of the basic materialism of the human condition and how we can learn from it.

Bataille is also inclined toward Hegel's doctrine of absolute dismemberment, that is, the heterogeneous nature of what can be known. Hegel claims that the Absolute Spirit realizes its own truth when it is in a condition of absolute dismemberment. Bataille incorporates this phrase in speaking of his own personal vision: "The atheistic mystic, *self-conscious,* conscious of having to die and to disappear, would live, as Hegel *obviously said concerning himself,* 'in absolute *dismemberment.*' "[15] Bataille incorporates Hegel's system into his own vision by bringing to the fore the fragmentary effect of human anxiety and displacing the rule of Hegel's Absolute Spirit or the teleology of the dialectic being drawn toward synthetic resolutions. Bataille learned Hegel through the mediation of Kojève's lectures, which, as Jean-Michel Besnier characterizes them, portrayed "anguish, struggle, and work as the constituent factors of humanity."[16]

Of course, Hegel is only one among many inclinations for Bataille. Since Bataille did not see himself as a "true philosopher" (OC, IV, 365), the philosophical work of Hegel must be seen as incorporated within the opus of Bataille the writer. Bataille's friend Maurice Blanchot views Hegel in Bataille from such a vantage point: ". . . here is a writer free to create a world without slaves, a world in which the slave, having become a master, founds the new law: thus, through writing, the enchained human immediately obtains freedom personally and for the world; such a person denies all that one is to become what one is not."[17] In contrast to Hegel's sadness before death because of his need to absorb the negative within the movement of a teleological synthesis and the totalizing Absolute Spirit, the slave is a model for Bataille of the joy before death, in the sense of becoming "what one is not." While Bataille acknowledges that Hegel's general focus is appealing in that "Hegel's philosophy is a philosophy of death—or of atheism" (OC, XII, 328), Bataille turns Hegel against Hegel[18] by turning the focus of this negative of the negative toward a social context. Emile Durkheim provides this perspective as well as the return to the sacred, which in Hegel is too transcendent (e.g., in the Absolute Spirit or the teleology of the dialectic). Let us look now at how Durkheim's sociological program attenuates the Hegelian influence in Bataille.

## Durkheim: The Social and the Sacred

Emile Durkheim (1858–1917) is regarded as the principal founder of modern sociology. Arguing for a rigorous social science dedicated to the study of society as a collective conscience, Durkheim also studies the role of the sacred for group identification. This relationship between the sacred and the social is one of the main questions for Bataille. Throughout his life and his writings, Bataille returns to either or both of these issues. Often he is concerned with how they affect each other. From Durkheim, Bataille views society as "a composite being" (OC, II, 295). Hence, the composition of society itself intrigues Bataille, especially insofar as the attitudes of the members of the group toward what they regard as sacred compose their identity as a particular social entity. These attitudes are often worked into a myth or story that the group narrates. For example, Bataille's efforts with various groups such as the *Collège de Sociologie,* the secret society *Acéphale,* and the Society for Collective Psychology often involved meetings in which the members discussed what they respected as sacred, that is, to what they had common allegiance.

Bataille's attitudes toward sacrifice, ritual, and myth owe much to the precedence of Durkheim's conception of the social as a function of a collective consciousness. Bataille elaborates upon the nature of the collective enterprise. Myth, as the narrative about the origins or the nature of a community, is crucial to the spiritual or religious expression of a group. The presence of sacrifice and ritual in many of the myths narrated within societies is also noteworthy in Bataille's construction of the nature of group identity. Bataille recognizes the centrality of myth in all this: "Myth is, together with the sacred, plainly one of the essential movements within the religious life; with the sacred it lies at the heart of all that has been analyzed by philosophy under the form of participation" (Richardson, *Absence,* 75). "Participation" for Bataille allows for the heterogeneity of those involved. Although the sacred may have a common meaning for those who contribute to and believe in the myth, Bataille also views the sacred as a means for creating new beings by the communication that takes place. At one point, he even defines the sacred as "the communication between beings and through this the formation of new beings" (OC, II, 371). Thus, as Durkheim would allow, a society is more than the sum of its individual components. In fact, the communication and participation in a common notion of the sacred promote the growth and the development of new persons. Bataille, in the spirit of Durkheim's scientific rigor, looks at biology for a model. There, he sees the phenomenon of schizogenesis (**la scissiparité**) whereby cells are divided to form new entities. Intellectually and socially, communities offer new lives to individuals who were not so involved prior to belonging to the community.

Bataille also adds to Durkheim's conception of the sacred as antiutilitarian and antipsychological. Whereas for Durkheim the sacred is dynamically representative of various groups, Bataille adapts the etymology of *sacer* in its medieval ambivalence meaning "sacred" and "syphilitic."[19] Given Bataille's base materialism and his father's disease, this key word *sacer* positions the experience of the sacred within mysticism and base materialism, which Bataille develops as symbiotic principles emanating from the social. This dualism is part of the life of nonknowledge, which continues Durkheim's rejection of utility and psychology and generates the negative theology of Bataille, that is, his atheology that he admits "as an effect of nonknowledge is knowable as are laughter and the sacred" (OC, VIII, 229).

This nonknowledge that is knowable is found by studying the intersections of the sacred and the social. These intersections lead Bataille to the methodological heritage of Durkheim, the rigorous scientific attitude that enables Bataille to assert during one of his lectures in the *Collège de Sociologie*: "The social core is in fact taboo, that is, untouchable and unnameable; from the beginning, it has the same character as cadavers, menstrual blood, and pariahs" (OC, II, 310). For Bataille taboo thus participates in the sacred and in fact grounds the Hegelian method of negation as a positive affirmation of collective identity. Although some of Bataille's readers such as Michael Richardson (in his *Georges Bataille*) see Bataille's primary affiliation as a sociologist, Bataille himself shunned the title and preferred to be a "sorcerer's apprentice."[20] In this latter identity, we can see him looking over the shoulder of one of Durkheim's principal disciples, Marcel Mauss, who continued Durkheim's influence by studying the magic through the combination of sociology and anthropology to produce what he called ethnology. Bataille speaks of Durkheim from a distance by reflecting: "I move away from his doctrine but not without retaining its essential character" (OC, VII, 358). Let us look at how Mauss inclined Bataille away from Durkheim in a shift toward economics.

## Mauss: Potlatch and the Theory of the Gift

Marcel Mauss (1872–1950), Durkheim's nephew, brought considerable prestige to Durkheim's social theories. They collaborated on a number of works, for example, *Le Suicide* (1897). However, Mauss's interests in anthropology also shifted his focus toward ethnology, a combination of anthropology and sociology, for which he founded in 1925 at l'Institut d'Ethnologie in Paris. Mauss is still well known because of his influence on structuralist writers like Claude Lévi-Strauss.[21] Mauss's studies of magic and potlatch among the Native American tribes of the Northwest led to his essay on gifts (1925) that became a crucial work for Bataille and others. While Bataille's associates Michel Leiris, Roger Caillois, Jules Monnerot, and Alfred Métraux (OC, XI, 58) took courses with Mauss, Métraux introduced Bataille to Mauss's work, which diverted Bataille's attention toward ethnology and economics.[22] The issue of economics has to do with the gift as a social principle of exchange and contract with assumptions about return and balance as governing the economic mind-sets of social groups. Bataille took these assumptions to be wrongheaded because of his own postulate of a general economy within which expense, rather than balance, is the governing assumption. Nevertheless, Mauss inspired Bataille to investigate ethnology for its insights into the relationships among sociology, anthropology, and economics.

In many ways, Mauss was marginalized, similar to Bataille himself, who conducted his writing career outside traditional universities. Mauss's lectures were given at the *École Pratique des Hautes Études,* an intellectual forum distinct from the conventional university setting such as the Sorbonne. Bataille never held a university position. His erudition was earned in the margins of a professorial community. In later life, at least, Mauss received the recognition of being elected to the prestigious Collège de France. Bataille was always disappointed not to enjoy popular acceptance of his work during his lifetime. Nevertheless, Bataille found Mauss's reflections fascinating. As the sorcerer's apprentice, Bataille looked over Mauss's shoulder to identify him as "perhaps the most remarkable interpreter of history" (OC, X, 68). Hence Mauss offered Bataille the opportunity to prove that Hegel was wrong in claiming the end of history. However, history according to Bataille would be different, a history that must address the issues of the exchanges that undergird society.

Through Mauss's studies of Melanesian, Polynesian, and northwest Native American societies, similar forms of exchange appeared common to them all. The tradition of potlatch, a practice by which heritage is assumed through gift giving and the distribution of valuables, was identified as a crucial form of economic exchange. Mauss's "Essay on the Gift" elaborates that such practices make a case for exchange as a basis for the postulate of an economic bond for a social entity.[23] Lévi-Strauss then based a theory of the incest taboo on Mauss's model and noted that in many societies women are similarly exchanged to achieve economic stability. This theory by Lévi-Strauss was seen by Bataille as an explanation of personal interest and generosity (OC, X, 231, n. 1) rather than of economic equilibrium in society. Bataille recognizes with Mauss and Lévi-Strauss the crucial role of gift giving as an economic principle for society. However, he disagrees with them regarding its ultimate effect. Mauss's theory of potlatch assumes a Hegelian harmony in which a symmetrical model results from the gift, since the subjects Mauss observed involved their soul in the exchange because they thought their soul (as well as the effect of the gift) would come back to them later.[24] Instead, Bataille posits pure expense as the ruling principle in a general economy. Where Bataille differs from Mauss is when he introduces production/consumption as a crucial element in the economy of gifts. Potlatch is, for Bataille, "the consumption for others" (OC, VII, 72), that is, pure expense in that it is an asymmetrical act in which the return cannot be assured. No matter the intent of the giver of the inheritance, in the case of potlatch, what the heiress or heir will do with the inheritance cannot be assured. In effect, Bataille portrays Mauss as condemning modern humanity "to a purely symbolic reconstruction of a past irretrievably lost" (Richman, *Reading*, 15). The exchanges that constitute the past cannot privilege the present or the future. However, Bataille looks toward Karl Marx to modify Mauss's view of history with an economic model that can be materialistic while offering the possibility for a mystical transaction within the social communication with the sacred.

## Marx: Economics and Dialectical Materialism

Hegel's dialectic offered Bataille an attractive portrayal of the slave that was nevertheless too limiting with its teleological orientation. Bataille looks toward Karl Marx, especially the young Marx's writings, for an alternative to Hegel's teleology. In refusing transcendent principles such as Hegel's Absolute Spirit, Marx adapts Hegel's dialectic to the materialistic operation of class struggle within a general, rather than a specific, economy. This general economy inspires Bataille to write on economics and to develop his vision of materialist expenditure as the primary principle for all economics. Bataille is not Marxist, but rather Marxian; that is, Bataille adapts the writings rather than the political agenda of perpetual revolution of Marx. Bataille still respected the subversion of authority and dominant systems within his economics of expenditure. Bataille saw, however, an ethical basis for his economics that included the political order and is more inclusive by affecting the values that humans have with each other.

Marx's theory of *surplus value,* the difference between the value of a product of labor and the wages paid for it, influenced Bataille's rejection of profit and savings within the capitalist scheme of economics. Marx comments that the capitalist exploits the worker through surplus value. During the 1930s, many Marxists claimed Marx as the alternative to capitalism and fascism. Bataille saw the problems of both capitalism and fascism. Even the Marxists were problematic because they did not recognize, in their antifascist mania to organize a Marxist government, "the fundamental problem of the State" (OC, I, 335). Bataille saw communism, one of the adaptations of Marx that seems closest to Bataille's view of sovereignty,[25] as a utopian promotion of abundance and thus the greed of surplus value. Instead, he advocated expenditure so that capital could be dissipated among the needy and shared with the masses.

The historical Marx haunted Bataille. In *Le Bleu du ciel*, Troppmann imagines Trier as the place where Marx had been as a child. In visiting the town, Troppmann wonders how Marx might have judged the Nazi children playing there in the 1930s "with so much violence" (OC, III,

486). These children predict the end of a historical Marx in that their violence represents the will for fascist assimilation. Bataille's vision is a restructuring of Marx because, in Hollier's words, "As an orthodox disciple of Kojève, Bataille took the concept of the end of history literally: if the class struggle is inherent in man's humanity, man will die as soon as he ceases to oppose himself, as soon as he does without differing or difference."[26] This is death in its material sense, a materialism that Marx envisioned as the economic and social determination of the human condition. Bataille would have materialism be an even more basic component of what he identifies as gnosis (**le gnosis**), that is, a form of knowledge of mysteries identified with spiritual truth. Marx is so opposed to organized religion that religion can be useful only as an "opiate of the masses." Not so for Bataille, for whom gnosis and base materialism must be linked, as he observes: "It is possible to identify as a leitmotif of gnosis the conception of matter as an *active* principle" (OC, I, 223). While Marx sees class struggle and the hope for change in the historical setting of dialectical materialism, Bataille views a mystical source of communication for individuals in the material recognition of death and the base materialism associated with it. Bataille recognizes with Marx that "in history as in nature, decay is the laboratory of life" (OC, II, 93). The vision of what constitutes life distinguishes the role of materialism for Marx and Bataille.

Marx, like Bataille, is also a critic of political economy. Especially in his work with Engels, Marx criticizes the capitalist economy's focus on consumption and looks toward production as a key ingredient in a socialist or communist society. But even Marx's proposal for a worldwide socialist revolution is too specific an economy for Bataille. Bataille advocated a general economy of expenditure in which interest, especially economic interest, would not be so compelling even as it is in communism. Bataille remarked that the specific government of Marxism has made interest an issue once again: "The fact that the Revolution developed in a backward country has been a crucial factor serving to compel Communism to rely in the most oppressive way on the value of economic interest" (Richardson, *Absence,* 77). And yet Marx's writings inspired Bataille to develop a general economy that could work to dispel surplus value and to produce change and subversion of the master's rule.

Bataille admired Marx's insights into class struggle. Indeed, for Bataille, "Class struggle becomes . . . the most grandiose form of social expense . . . which threatens the very existence of masters" (OC, I, 316). The negative principle of Hegel's dialectic as well as the principle of the sovereignty of humanity are preserved in the class struggle. Bataille identified with the need of the masses to be sovereign[27] and especially focused, in his work with *Contre-Attaque,* on workers to struggle for that right: "We focus on their human instinct not to bow their head before anything, on their moral freedom, and on their violence" (OC, I, 382). Violence is condoned here as a means to assert human sovereignty. However, although Bataille realized that Marx promoted the proletarian rise to power during a time when the numbers of proletarians were increasing, Bataille likewise acknowledged that the proletariat was not extensive enough in numbers to overwhelm the established regimes (OC, I, 414). Perhaps this dose of political reality in the late 1930s turned Bataille away from his active participation in Marxist endeavors. Nevertheless, Bataille did turn toward more religious issues during the mid-1930s and eventually turned away from Marx.

One of the liabilities in Marx's writings is his lack of attention to the spiritual, a crucial human component for Bataille. In Marx's enthusiasm to undermine the powers of organized religion, which even Bataille rejected after his pious phase, he rashly relegated religion to a means of controlling the masses. Bataille refers to Marx's phrase of the "opiate of the masses" and turns it differently: "The opiate of the people in the present-day world is perhaps not so much religion as accepted boredom" (OC, I. 410). There are still some very important personal, communicative, and social roles for religion that Marx overlooks. Hence, Bataille looked elsewhere and found the work of Max Weber to be very compelling for what it offered to Bataille's own mystical vision that owes much to Marx.

## Weber: Calvinism and the Ethics of Accumulation

Max Weber (1864–1920) was a German economist and social historian who was influenced by Marx's principles of historical determinism and who integrated ethical and religious factors within economic considerations. Weber's explanations of the ethics of accumulation within capitalism effectively gave Bataille the economic system against which he would develop economic alternatives. By reading Weber, Bataille found an explanation for the economic problems of accumulation, surplus value, and utility. Weber's *The Protestant Ethic and the Spirit of Capitalism* (1904–1905) is a classic study in the sociology of religion whereby the values of Calvinism and Lutheranism are placed within the development of capitalism. Bataille agreed with Weber's general observation that such a Protestant ethic promotes the accumulation of capital through the "iron cage" of its bureaucratic implementation. However, Bataille's *La Part maudite* (1949) is dedicated to proposing a totally different economic system. Although Bataille admits being "somewhat opposed to Max Weber's spirit" (OC, VII, 122) by going counter to the bureaucratic capitalist spirit of accumulation, he does admit that the Reformation had a major role in determining the bourgeois links between utility and the growth of wealth by instilling "the morality of commerce" (OC, VII, 118). Where Bataille disagrees with Weber is in the recognition of the influence of the Reformation's morality of commerce. While Weber identifies historical causality in the melding of Reformation work ethic and capitalist greed, Bataille prefers to see the development of "the fiction of useful activity" (OC, VII, 222). Bataille calls into question the easy claim to usefulness as the principle upon which economic explanations should be made.

Weber also extends his study of institutionalized Reformation religions into larger claims about human spirituality. Bataille takes exception to some of these ties. He does not agree with Weber's rationalistic claim for "the great historic process in the development of religions, the elimination of magic from the world . . . came ... to its logical conclusion" in the Protestant ethic.[28] Bataille goes back to ancient religions to study rituals of magic and the practices of sacrifice and adds to Weber, as we shall see, Pascal's spiritual arguments for belief in magic despite the apparently invasive and sure paths of mathematical certainty.

Weber does a valuable service by identifying for Bataille what has to be transgressed. Weber's historical studies are found wanting as too restricted in economic breadth when he addresses ancient societies or those of the Eastern world. Bataille was attracted to societies where sacrifice, loss, and expenditure are operative economic principles because of what they tell Western and Christian systems about their restrictions. Weber's links between religion and economics were a valuable precedent as Bataille examines the cults of sacrifice in religious rituals among the Aztecs and other ancient societies. Bataille's insights, nonetheless, led him away from Weber's conclusions about a restricted capitalist economy of greed and toward an economy of loss in which the sovereignty of giving without receiving reigns based upon the model of the energy from the sun (OC, VII, 35). Hence, as Weber shows, ethics, religion, and economics are intertwined in strange fashions. From these distant cultures, Bataille preferred to study religion because, for him, "Religion responds in general to the universal human desire to find oneself and to recover an intimacy that has always been strangely displaced" (OC, VII, 122). So Pascal and Unamuno modify Weber's sense of religion for Bataille. A particular institutional religion is too much a piece of fiction for Bataille. As he cast aside the Catholic model, likewise did the Reformed Christian model seem too narrow in its focus. Pascal and Unamuno provide Bataille with wider breadth in their inclinations.

## Pascal and Unamuno: The Other Side of the Wager

Blaise Pascal (1623–1662) and Miguel de Unamuno (1864–1936) offered their religious inclinations to Bataille's respect for noninstitutionalized spiritual experiences. On the one hand, Pascal is the mathematician who loved gambling and enjoyed a frivolous life, as Bataille was reputed to have led when in Paris. Pascal's wager about the existence of God indicates that God exists or doesn't exist at the flip of a coin. This wager places the believer on the brink of the abyss of human anxiety, which fascinated Bataille so. On the other hand, Unamuno is the twentieth-century forerunner of existentialist concerns, and within Bataille one reads echoes of Unamuno's reflections on suffering, human anguish, the impossible (**l'impossible**), the role of the community in religious ritual, impotence (both physical and existential), mysticism, and Tibetan transcendental meditation. Whereas Unamuno was an authentic believer who was skeptical about his faith, Bataille tended to be less rationalistic and more mystical in his religious temperament. It is almost as if Bataille decided to be the other side of the coin to Unamuno's skepticism. Both Unamuno and Pascal appealed to Bataille because they admitted that their religious crises were ongoing, which thus placed them on the edge of the abyss of human anxiety.

Like Bataille, Pascal had an attraction for science, the certitude with which human beings can know anything. This curiosity for science—mathematics for Pascal and economics and anthropology for Bataille—is close to both of their skeptical attitudes about the existence of God. They were both searching and struggling with their religious instincts for something that was other than human and yet was based in the human body and its desires to get beyond itself. Pascal's interest in gambling while in Paris is purported to be linked to his later scientific writings on probability theory and calculus. However, like Unamuno, Pascal opts for belief and hence does not have that sense of groundlessness that Bataille experiences as he peers over the yawning abyss of nothingness. Bataille learned to appreciate Pascal, along with Nietzsche, Dostoyevsky, and Kierkegaard, from Leon Chestov in Paris during the early 1920s when Bataille was undergoing a transformation from his pious, Catholic faith in God. Michel Surya, in his biography of Bataille, portrays Bataille as learning from Chestov to appreciate the "nietzscheanized Pascal" (Surya, 83). So Bataille learned to admire the suffering, the hesitation, and the doubts in Pascal's scientific wager.

Similarly, the mixture of reflection on the sacred and a concern for science might also have brought Heidegger closer to Bataille. Heidegger, however, cloaks his curiosity for the sacred within a philosophical vocabulary that appears to be profane. Bataille admits that he did not have anything other than "a nervous attraction" for Heidegger (OC, IV, 365). Some readers of Bataille, such as Steven Shaviro, go even further and point out "Bataille's profound revulsion for Heidegger."[29] Clearly, Bataille disassociates himself from Heidegger, for whatever reason and despite some interesting parallels regarding the roles of technology, care, and community.

Bataille's travel to Spain in 1922 brought him to the land where Unamuno's crises with his faith found a sympathetic ear. Unamuno's *The Tragic Sense of Life in Men and Nations* appeared in 1913, was translated widely by 1921, and contains much of the skepticism and uncertainty that Bataille himself was beginning to experience about his own faith. Like Pascal, Unamuno was a believer in God, although he struggled more with that belief. Like the later Bataille, Unamuno speaks about atheology, the abyss of nothingness, the suffering and anguish of not knowing, the impossible, his intellectual impotence, and concerns with Tibetan forms of transcendental meditation and mysticism. Bataille returned from Spain and a short while thereafter renounced his faith and began developing thoughts, similar to those expounded by Unamuno, into the components of an atheology. Unamuno, also influenced by Nietzsche, viewed science as an opponent of faith and a component of atheology. For Unamuno, "Positivism brought us an age of rationalism, that is of materialism, mechanism, or mortalism; and thus it is that now vitalism, spiritualism, return to the scene."[30] And Bataille unites base materialism with the spiritualism that he calls atheological almost as if he were developing the other side of the belief to which Unamuno clings despite his doubts. Also inclining toward Bataille, Unamuno brings together reflections on ethics and economics to remark that "this economic order is essentially nothing but an inchoate religious order" (Unamuno, 345). Bataille provides a vision of economics in which there is ethical order for the community at large. Certainly, Bataille leaves behind the faith of Unamuno, as well as that of Pascal. In addition,

Bataille's writings are much more expansive and visionary than Unamuno's. Nonetheless, Bataille returned from Spain ready to write and to begin his prolific career with much to say about theology without God. Let us now look at the kinds of things he wrote so that we may appreciate the breadth and depth of his distinctive vision.

## *Chapter Three*

# More Than One Face

In his self-consciousness as a writer, Georges Bataille explored many variations for his art. While he acknowledged that "literature is consumption" (OC, XII, 26) and that he was never as widely read during his lifetime as he would have liked, he did publish novels, poetry, and essays; edit journals; and write on political and scientific matters. Bataille admits that "in the final analysis, I have more than one face, and I don't know which one is laughing at the other" (OC, VI, 83). The laughter is his means of not privileging one type of writing over another. Laughter is also an outlet for fear ("If you laugh, it's because you are afraid" [OC, III, 15]). The fear has to do with the phenomenon of impotence, a strong intellectual and physical fear in Bataille. Some of his characters, such as the naked Eponine, who talks constantly in *L'Abbé C.* (OC, III, 321), and Henri Troppmann, who is sexually impotent with Dirty in *Le Bleu du ciel*, express various modes of his own insecurity. Bataille writes in *Eroticism* that to speak is to reveal one's own impotence (OC, X, 242). For Bataille, writing is one way to speak and to express his anguish about his discontinuity (**la discontinuité**) with others. His narratives and his poetry both reflect the paradoxes of his personal and social concerns.

Bataille's various attempts to set up narratives are thrusts toward establishing continuity among all the fragments around him. Like his character Charles in *L'Abbé C.*, Bataille could say that the secret of literature lies in its power to recall the "traces of death" (OC, III, 336) because of literary writing's recollection in the face of the absolute discontinuity and effacement of death. Bataille's narratives especially bear witness to traces of the ultimate discontinuity of death and, as Denis Hollier describes, "reopen a hole, point out a hole, a grotto"[1] in what appeared to be the solid firmament of life and its affirmations. Bataille reveals the anxiety and vertigo of living on the edge of the abyss, which in *Le Bleu du ciel* Troppmann calls "a black hole within myself" (OC, III, 430), in which is expressed his "state of impotence" (OC, III, 444). Throughout his writings, Bataille explores his own discomfort, expressed by Troppmann thus: "I was obsessed with this hole" (OC, III, 450) within my self. Bataille's writings implement poetic variations about the energy found in this internal void, sometimes expressed as obsessions with the sun (OC, III, 455), the corolla of a flower (OC, I, 175), or the ovoid form (*L'Histoire de l'oeil*, 1927), but much more powerfully in what Hollier identifies as "the subversive power of the anecdotal . . . such as to prevent the world from reaching completion."[2] This power of Bataille's writing is also an antiarchitectural tendency[3] because not only is completion denied but also any teleological or organizational structure linking the material of this life to a transcendental cause or purpose. Religion is, nevertheless, an abiding interest to Bataille the writer, who is intent upon retaining the ritual of sacrifice in his writing's subversive power. Hence, as Sylvère Lotringer portrays this Nietzschean writing, Bataille must be "furiously Christian"[4] to sacrifice God to base materialism in such a ritualized way.

Bataille curiously adopts many pseudonyms, especially in his creative and pornographic writings, as he implements this sacrifice of God. The pseudonyms of Bataille have been identified as Lord Auch (*L'Histoire de l'oeil*), Pierre Angélique (*Madame Edwarda* and *Le Mort*), Louis Trente (*Le Petit*), and Dianus (*Le Coupable*, *L'Alleluiah: Catéchisme de Dianus*, and "Histoire des rats"). His self-masking behind these pseudonyms is an involvement in literary playfulness as Bataille avoids the truthfulness of his own identity. And yet Bataille complains about his writings being too facilely ascribed to a literary mode (OC, VII, 19) because the writings themselves defy the generic classification of Bataille within a single category. Michael Richardson would have us believe that "to write was for Bataille as a taboo experience" (Richardson, *Bataille,* 63) in that the subject is involved in a nonscientific way with the object being described. Indeed, this is the myth that Bataille reintroduces with his writing. Anguish is at the very core of his vision of "perpetual questioning."[5] Bataille's anguished questioning often returns us, with him, to a phenomenon whereby "literature identifies itself with that guilty childhood we might describe as a 'major' childhood: it wastes no time defending itself" (Hollier, *Tomb,* 97). Instead, Bataille brings his reader into the anguish between childhood and adulthood as he readily admits that the writer who takes the glory of literary work as the fulfillment of destiny could be fooled (OC, I, 525). One of Bataille's recurring concerns is the "sliding into impotence of a thought which is expressed in literature" (OC, VIII, 583). Nevertheless, Bataille's literary output is before us.

## Provocative Fiction

Georges Bataille's narratives have often been called pornographic. This word is a catchall for those attributes of his narratives that shock with their frank sexuality, violence, and confrontation with death. Perhaps provocative better describes the effect of Bataille's novels, which include *L'Histoire de l'oeil* (1928), *Le Bleu du ciel* (written in 1935 and published in 1957), *Madame Edwarda* (1941), *L'Abbé C.* (1950), *Ma Mère* (1966), and *Le Mort* (1967). There are also many significant, short pieces of fiction that serve to establish Bataille's identity as a creative writer of narratives. Among the most crucial are "W.C." (written in 1924 and destroyed by Bataille), "Le Petit" (1934), and a series of narratives appearing in 1947—*Le Coupable*, *L'Alleluiah: Le Catéchisme de Dianus*, and "l'Histoire des rats." His fictional writing is often outrageous, but not simply because of its transgressions of social guidelines about what is taboo. Bataille's fiction stays with his reader because of the bold situations of humanity confronting its sexuality, violence, and death. Bataille's vision ranges from youthful eroticism involving ovoid shapes in *L'Histoire de l'oeil*, to the death of a father and the mother's ensuing incestuous seduction of her son in *Ma Mère*, and to death itself and the eroticism it suggests in *Le Bleu du ciel* and *Le Mort*. Yukio Mishima, the Japanese writer whose own writings struggle with the problems and ties between sexuality and death, admires Bataille's "novels of degradation (taking place)."[6] It is exactly the degradation of human nature to its base materialism that is at play in these novels and that so provokes Bataille's reader. To call this type of writing pornographic is too facile because the term dismisses his novels as immoral and unworthy of reflection. On the contrary, his novels are not facile pornography, not acts of violence toward women with the goal of making women disappear relative to men,[7] not mere dreams of fantasy unconnected to the community of men and women, and not acts of disrespect for the human condition.

What Bataille's novels do offer are provocative readings (**la provocation**) about how fantasy can provoke us into uncanny involvements with others. The word *uncanny* is used deliberately here for its reference to Freud, for whom humor and the uncanny hold a special relationship. Bataille also has a healthy respect for the importance of humor in relieving the stress of anxiety. In the foreword to *Le Bleu du ciel*, Bataille notes that narratives "reveal the multiple truth of life" (OC, III, 380) through the eyes of an author whose vision is not constrained. Hence, the frank violence, sexuality, presence of death, and laughter generated by this "uncanny" mixture allow Bataille to present a literary vision governed by fiction. Fiction offers alternatives for meaning in an age when science appears to have a firm grasp on "truth." Bataille qualifies this firm grasp by noting that "the truth striven for by science is true only if it is devoid of meaning, and nothing has any meaning unless it is fiction."[8] Laughter allows Bataille to separate the scientific judgment of his novels as pornographic[9] from the fictional realm of provocative writing whereby he can claim that "literature is communication [which is] a sovereign operation" (OC, IX, 306). It is Bataille the writer who is sovereign in providing humor to relieve the scientific seriousness of judging as pornographic the mixture of violence, sexuality, and death. Bataille prefers that his novels communicate to his writers and provoke them into thinking differently than they have been.

*L'Histoire de l'oeil*, first published anonymously in 1927 under the name of Lord Auch, proves to be especially challenging as a literary document. The first-person narrator is an adolescent male who meets Simone, a 16-year-old woman with unusual fascinations with the ovoid form. The pair's experiences together constitute an erotic bildungsroman whereby they, and their teenage peer group, come of age together through various tests of what is taboo regarding sexuality, death, violence, and religion. Their challenges to the sacred provoke by going far beyond the limits of the dreamworld and become experiments in fantasy and even nightmare.

One of their friends, Marcelle, has a fascination with being enclosed in a stand-up armoire. The image of Marcelle in her armoire recalls Bataille's portrayal, in *L'Erotisme* (1957), of the enclosed restrictions of taboo and the transgression of those restrictions by the various practices of eroticism. Marcelle's freedom from her anguished enclosure is allied with her anguished eroticism and ultimately her suicide, thus predicting what Bataille would write in *L'Erotisme*: "While we experience the anguished desire of being delivered from this which is perishable, we are obsessed with a primary continuity, which generally ties us back to being" (OC, X, 20). In effect, the consciousness of death is anticipated by "the endearing, dead" (**le petit mort**) moment of sexual pleasure. Bataille is fascinated with the French idiom linking sexuality and death. In *Histoire de l'oeil*, as with many of his subsequent narratives, death and eroticism are juxtaposed, and eroticism is even heightened by the proximity of death. The character of Marcelle is caught in her anguish about the links between death and eroticism. Marcelle's struggles with her body, her life, and her freedom are all portrayed in her fantasies within an enclosed armoire. Her eroticism is typically practiced alone within this armoire, and her suicide is the final expression of the solitude that denies her existence with others. Marcelle's eroticism and her untimely death are haunting prefigurations of Bataille's later reflection in *L'Erotisme* that

". . . sexuality is damned . . . insofar as it deviates from its function of multiplying human beings" (OC, X, 652). Of course, this is society's myth about sexuality. Reproduction does not happen with Marcelle, nor with Simone, the narrator Lord Auch, or any of the major characters in the story. Children are left behind in that the story is about the transition from childhood to adulthood through sexual fantasies and their realization or repression.

In *L'Histoire de l'oeil*, sexual fantasy contests the sacred. The sacred is adapted therein from the law of the father, the nurturing presence of the mother, and the representation of the sacred by the Church.[10] The absence of the narrator's mother and father is a challenge to the sacredness of their presence for the child.[11] However, the presence of violent and erotic acts as well as sacrileges to a priest (Don Aminado) and the blasphemous attitudes of the adolescent characters toward institutionally sacred objects such as the Host, the consecrated wine, and a ciborium is a direct challenge by youth to the nature of the sacred. Andrea Dworkin takes exception to Bataille's story as a pornographic tale directed against women and portrays the priest episode thus: "The priest as the man in skirts, feminized because he has turned away from masculine sexual action as a way of life, is easily viewed as a symbol of repression caused by religion, whereas it would be more realistic—but less comfortable—to see him as a substitute woman" (Dworkin, 175). Perhaps the sacredness of essentialist conventions about who women are may also be at stake if one agrees with Dworkin's view of *L'Histoire de l'oeil* as pornography. However, there is even more at stake within this story.

The nature of representation itself is being questioned by Bataille through his focus on the visual. The narrative is playing with forming the question asked in *Madame Edwarda*: "What does truth mean outside the representation of excess if we don't see what exceeds the possibility of seeing . . . ?" (OC, III, 12). In other words, are there truths other than the ones that are seen? If so, what is the value of the truths that are seen? Are observed truths just fantasies of the imagination or the only sources of meaning we have? As the narrator responds to Simone's obsession with ovoid forms, "This interrogation could not remain without an answer" (OC, I, 39). The adolescents in the story are not concerned with metaphysical questions, nor with their answers. However, their responses to and involvements with each other's fantasies appear to be examples of what Bataille calls the "prickly eye" (**l'oeil pinéal**), an expression capturing the French play on the relationship between a male erection and its visual inducement by both fantasy and direct observation. Does the penis influence what the eye sees, or vice versa? An eye on the head of a penis is an obscenity even for Bataille (OC, II, 416) and yet also a fascination as the possible alternative for the overbearing presence of the sun, another image that haunts, in surrealist fashion (e.g., the image of a urinating sun or the omnipresent sun in Spain as an eye able to see everything, thus precluding the ability to hide any taboo). In one of Bataille's surrealist poems ("Rêve"), he appropriately comments that "the prickly eye . . . [is] an irresistible desire for oneself to become the *sun*" (OC, II, 14). As the adolescents of his story step and urinate upon the grave of Don Juan in Seville, they too are looking for other models for their sexuality and must desecrate what is no longer efficacious in their estimation. And Bataille the writer likewise matures and produces other narratives that reflect the interests of other stages in human life.

*Le Bleu du ciel* is a fine narrative dedicated to impotence, both sexual and intellectual. The title refers not only to the infinite openness of the blue sky but also to the bruise of abstract thinking to the base materialism of human existence (*le bleu* refers to a mark left by a hard blow to the skin, as with a black eye). The narrator, Troppmann, introduces ideas that develop some of the concerns in *L'Histoire de l'oeil*. Anguish, laughter, and the hiccup are often associated with discussions of impotence, virility, and its various guises for human relationships.

Once again, the ambience is marked by the presence of Spain's sun with its unremitting light and heat. Some commentators find this narrative to be a political novel (Hollier, *Tomb,* 86 ff.) debating the merits of literature and communism. However, the sweltering, blinding sun also influences the breakdown of relationships. Nature will have its way. Troppmann's marriage to Emily is dissolving, and he takes up with Dirty, a beautiful woman who encounters Troppmann's impotence. Troppmann tries to be "too much of a man" (*trop* means "too much"); in other words, he fails at virility before the incarnation of female pulchritude. He cannot be a male when the female is daunting and challenging him to perform. With the women Lazare (recalling the New Testament survivor of death) and Xénie, who are not as overwhemingly beautiful as Dirty, Troppmann is more comfortable and is not as plagued by "my impotent status" (OC, III, 444). His impotence is not merely a male sexual problem, but a state of anguish that is a human affliction he describes metaphorically: "as if I fell into the abyss [**le vide**] with absurd gestures, as in a dream when we shoot ineffective [**impuissants**] gunfire" (OC, III, 445). This image of firing blanks recalls Breton's metaphor for the impact of surrealism as the surrealist artists aimlessly shooting into a crowd. However, Bataille's impotent narrator is shooting blanks, certainly quite the contrast to Troppmann's alternative of virility, a word common to other French novelists of the 1930s such as Malraux and Drieu la Rochelle. Certainly sexist images, both impotence and virility refer to sexual, moral, and political involvement. While their women partners were usually subordinated or even erased in their political situations, virile men were actively involved in their historical moments. These were the "new" men Sartre would later transform into his *engagés*. Bataille's Troppmann, however, cannot meet the demands of this highly charged, emotive individual. Emotionally, intellectually, and politically, Troppmann is impotent, not virile. He does not have the effectiveness of a human being among others. This effectiveness is the virility known to Bataille and his contemporaries, as Susan Rubin Suleiman (*Streets,* 34) expresses well: "To be virile is to be active, energetic, and courageous in matters private and public, and to be potent sexually." Note that the sexual meaning is last, as if it were the basis for what Suleiman calls the "sexual politics" of the 1930s. Hence, *Le Bleu du ciel* is once again read as a political novel. And yet it is the failure of a political model, in this case a sexist hierarchy rather than the communist ideals expounded by Troppmann's colleague Michel and Xénie about the revolution in Barcelona and proposed by Hollier as the effectiveness against which Troppmann analyzes his own ineptitude.

Failure is often at the core of the anguish of Bataille's literary characters. Troppmann's broken marriage, his sexual impotence, and his terror are all variations on failure. In the face of these failures, Troppmann bears witness to the sharing of his terror as an ultimate form of human communication: "For Bataille, indeed, human communication at its fullest—that which he names 'communication' or 'intimacy'—is sustained by the opening of the self to terror shared" (Michelson, 112). In *Le Bleu du ciel*, Michel says to Xénie that Lazare wanted him to put needles in her back so that Lazare could endure Michel's torture over his own impotence. But Michel dies in the Catalan revolution so that Lazare's metaphorical rise from the dead to share his anguish seems defeated. This view of shared torture recalls Bataille's own fascination with the photographs depicting the "100 forms of punishment" that Adrien Borel gave him in 1925 as part of his psychoanalytic treatment. Bataille believes in a mystical solidarity achieved by the ritualized, common experiences of pain and suffering.

Death, however, promises separation and finally separates the dead individual from others. After Michel's death, Troppmann finally makes love to Dirty in a cemetery under the stars where their ties to the anguish of death and eroticism are vividly described, as Bataille once again shows his own obsession with the little death of sexual pleasure. These ties between death and sexual pleasure are also relived in the Don Juan/Commendador myth reborn in the person of Troppmann, as Denis Hollier develops at length (*Tomb,* 73–102). The link between Don Juan, the myth of incarnate male eroticism, and the Commendador was introduced in *L'Histoire de l'oeil* with the blasphemous urination of the youths on the grave of Don Juan in Seville. Within the single character of Troppmann is found the ambivalence of Bataille toward the anguish of both eroticism and death. Guilt, which is a religious voice remaining from Bataille's Catholicism and not found in the dharma studied by Bataille in Hinduism and Buddhism, provides a haunting overlay to Troppmann's lasting anguish about the apparent ties found in the communication of realized sexual desire. Bataille returns to this with *Le Coupable* (1961) to reiterate that actually, as Denis Hollier says well, ". . . sex [is] an experience of what separates people" ("Tale," xii).

Dirty is a pet name for Dorothea. In her full name she acts defiantly to many myths other than Troppmann's virility. In Vienna, she spreads herself out in the form of a cross without the piety of praying. Effectively, she appears as a crucified Christ, but more importantly, she suggests herself as an available sexual partner. When Troppmann tells her that he doesn't understand why she would enter a church to do this, she replies: "If only you could lose your head" (OC, III, 477). Indeed, her blasphemy is not only a negative pastiche of a crucified Christ, but it also makes a claim for a nonrational, nonintellectualized religion of human eroticism, not only Troppmann's, but hers also. Bataille comments appropriately, in another context, about "the absolutely sovereign quality of this virility" (OC, II, 96). "This virility" is the visually obvious sign of an erection or male sexual desire. There is also Dorothea's side, which is not very distant from the presence of Laure in Bataille's life. It is crucial to recognize, with Jean-François Fourny, that "Laure haunts [*Le Bleu du ciel*] from one end to the other,"[12] that is, the erotic desire of *Le Bleu du ciel* is a human one and not simply a male struggle for power.

In Bataille's third novel, *L'Abbé C.* (1950), the religious undertones of human eroticism become explicit. Alfred, the narrator, has been told to edit the manuscript of Charles, who is telling the story of his brother, Robert, the Abbé C. Robert and Charles are twins, representing, perhaps, the two sides of mystical and base materialistic humanity. Robert is a lapsing priest, and Charles is suicidal. The title plays on the simplicity of the alphabet (a, b, c) and also that the priest might be Charles, since his name begins with a C. The priest, Robert, portrays himself as "laughing like an angel" (OC, III, 345) in the privacy of the enclosed toilet (the w.c.), yet he provokes others by dying of torture from the Nazis after having denounced his brother Charles and the prostitute Eponine. An earlier version of this narrative was entitled *Eponine*. Both narratives claim by their title to be about Charles's other, either his brother or his sexual partner. The premonition of Charles's suicide haunts Robert and Eponine from the moment they all climbed a church tower by mounting a ladder. This ladder, a metaphor for the human desire to ascend, be distinct, and escape from material nature, is also the means to climb out of the abyss of anxiety. Charles narrates how he falls or jumps from higher up the ladder into his brother Robert's arms: "Being suspended right over the abyss, having escaped death only by chance, I experienced the elation of this feeling of impotence" (OC, III, 257). This mixture of laughter, anguish, and communication about the anxiety of human life contrasts with the starkness of the priest's dedication to celibacy, prayer, and piety. And yet they are all combined, especially in the presence of Eponine, whose music-hall singing, sensual exuberance, and laughter in the face of piety express her Nietzschean "resentment" (OC, III, 271).

Robert has promised to his bishop to say his last Sunday Mass. After the promise, Charles and Eponine plan the sexual seduction of Robert. Eponine attends the Mass along with two women friends, Rosie and Raymonde. Eponine is constantly on the brink of laughter while Robert officiates at the Mass. Robert pretends to pass out after the *Kyrie Eleison*. The *Kyrie* is an exotic prayer, the only Greek part of the Mass, that alternately sings of the presence of God and Christ with the people. This prayer of divine presence, rather than transcendence, is an appropriate moment for the abbé to feign death, that is, to show within the religious ritual the end of his material existence. It is also crucial for Robert to pinch the arm of Charles and thus to convey "the necessity of not being dead" (OC, III, 309). Robert thus can laugh within the ritual and also make Charles, Eponine, and the other women laugh along with him.

Robert's betrayal of Charles and Eponine must be understood in the context of the narrator's presentation of Robert's spying on Charles and Eponine making love. Robert probably even defecated during the sexual tryst between Eponine and his brother. The pleasure of one brother is usually linked to that of the other; often one is on a religious and/or mystical plane while the other is on the level of sensual pleasure of one kind or another. Charles claims that "I couldn't, without speaking of myself, speak about how he would measure up" (OC, III, 327). And yet Eponine's speaking was about herself, especially "the naked Eponine spoke continuously" (OC, III, 273).

Words and nudity (**la nudité**) have a special relationship for Bataille. Michael Richardson (*Bataille,* 38) notes Bataille's insight that "when we are naked we are faced with the anguish of our origins and our incompleteness: naked, we contemplate an inadequacy at the heart of ourselves." Thus, Eponine expresses this human inadequacy. For Robert, however, it is speech itself that kept Charles at bay, as Charles notes that "Robert has been getting on my nerves for a long time because of a smiling verbosity, a mask which he obstinately wore to put off any possible intimacy" (OC, III, 271). That smile Robert used was a deliberate mask that perpetuated the separation between the twins, as with the two extremes of human experience, mysticism and base materialism. Charles's editor, the narrator Alfred, places Robert's final denouncement of Charles and Eponine to the Nazis in the category of a provocation rather than an admission. Perhaps the provocation is the continual separation of the twins, which seems to create anguish as well as relieve it. The religious ritual of the Mass brought together Robert, Charles, and Eponine in a ceremony of mutual communication that was never finished and perhaps never could be.

In a posthumously published narrative called "Julie," the association of laughter, death, and sexuality continues with a trio of friends. This time, two women (Julie and Suzanne) and a man (Henri, the brother of Suzanne) exchange provocations. Julie is a dancer at the Folies Bergères. Henri is suicidal in that "he felt himself to be laughable [while] he himself could no longer laugh" (OC, IV, 72). Julie is described as "improperly bathed" (*mal lavée* [OC, IV, 77]), thus recalling Dirty in *Le Bleu du ciel* in alluding to the base materialism that Bataille's anxious narrators sometimes associate with sexual partners. Julie is present with Suzanne around Henri's body after his attempted suicide. His impending death becomes for her "a door opening toward the impossible" (OC, IV, 103), that is, her sexual life lying before her, apparently inert. Suzanne, who hated her brother possibly because of his active sexual life with Julie, attacks Julie after also realizing that "how could one not know that he was a door opening toward the impossible?" (OC, IV, 114). Suzanne's violence is a manifestation of her own frustration with the links between eroticism and death, which Henri's anguish demonstrates to both women in his attempted suicide.

Bataille provokes even more poignantly with *Madame Edwarda*, another of his narratives published under a pseudonym, this time, that of "Pierre Angélique." Once again, we see Bataille's mask for himself, his guilty conscience hiding behind a persona. Susan Sontag (35–73) has argued that the 1956 preface to the third edition of this story is crucial to an understanding of its significance. However, Michael Richardson (*Bataille,* 62–63) points out that, while the third edition's authorship is still attributed to Pierre Angélique, the preface is written by Georges Bataille as a different persona speaking. This is a crucial literary insight uncharacteristic of Richardson, who usually displaces Bataille's literary talents in favor of the sociological vision of Bataille's writings. Bataille deliberately uses pseudonyms that mask the shame of his own socialization despite his atheological, mystical vision otherwise. In *Madame Edwarda* we read with Mark Taylor Bataille's "outrageous fiction,"[13] which calls analytical philosophy into question by making reason (i.e., Bataille's shame) turn itself inside out and spew out what it cannot look at. The word **méduser** (meaning to paralyze or to stupefy) is frequently used by Troppmann to speak of his own guilt about his necrophilia in *Le Bleu du ciel*. This word recalls the mythological figure of Medusa, the sorceress at whom no one could directly look for fear of being turned into stone. Bataille transforms her into Madame Edwarda, who invites her bordello patron to look directly at her most intimate parts and thus see her "divinity" without fear of losing his humanity.

The narrative *Madame Edwarda* is centered about Pierre Angélique's debauchery during his visit to a bordello near the Porte St.-Denis in Paris. The madam of the bordello is Madame Edwarda, who shows her vulva to the drunken patron with such extreme attention to detail that he must ask why. She replies, "so you can see that I am God" (OC, III, 22). Then, she invites him to look and to kiss her vulva rather than to debate and discuss why she is doing it. He does so and then recognizes that "I then knew—once every trace of drunkenness in me had worn off—that She had not lied, that She was God" (OC, III, 24). Madame Edwarda's invitation to touch and kiss her vulva recalls Christ's solicitation to the doubting Thomas. Only when Thomas places his hand into Christ's open wound does his faith in Christ as God manifest itself. Likewise, Pierre's touching Madame Edwarda's open wound convinces him of her divinity.

Madame Edwarda's "provoking position" (OC, III, 21) awakened in Pierre not simply his sexual appetite, but what Bataille later calls "a desire for nonknowledge" (OC, XII, 540). This status of nonknowledge has to do with how our human sexuality participates in both our base materialism and in our mystical being. Bataille claims that "a woman's vulva is sovereign: it is sacred but also laughable; she who allows it to be seen is degraded" (OC, XII, 286). This sovereignty effectively inverts the "position" of base materialism in the institutionalized, feudal view of sovereignty. Instead, Bataille points to the sovereignty of a woman's sexuality to break down the traditional hierarchy and to make her both divine and animal. While her desire is explained by the observation that "the delirium of being naked possessed her" (OC, III, 22), the concomitant questioning of this nakedness by Pierre Angélique reminds us, with Lucette Finas, that animals are not naked, but naked humans recall the animal nature in us all.[14]

The double vision of Madame Edwarda as god and human-animal is what makes her story, in Maurice Blanchot's words, "the most beautiful narrative of our time."[15] The beauty has to do with the story's ties between the extremes of human nature and how Bataille's nonknowledge recognizes this divergence as an exaltation, even an ecstatic vision, of what has been defined in the past as "disgusting" and "repugnant." The etymology of pornography as "writing about prostitution" is a telling one for Bataille because, as in *Madame Edwarda*, he investigates the nature of what it is that is being prostituted in such writing. Appropriately, in his later formal study of eroticism, Bataille claims that "fate has mandated that humanity laughs about its reproductive organs" (OC, X, 259–60). This laughter contributes to Bataille's nonknowledge, that mystical encounter that he develops in *L'Expérience intérieure* as being generated by a vision of communion between apparently disparate and heterogeneous components of being: "Communicating means trying to attain unity and being for many, one, which has succeeded in meaning the word 'communion' " (OC, VI, 279).

This communion is a religious ritual for Bataille. In the Catholic Mass, the ritual of communion is preceded by the reenactment of Christ's sacrifice. Likewise, Madame Edwarda's exhibitionism is an enactment of her own sacrificial status in the bordello, as Maurice Blanchot (*Communauté,* 80) describes it: "Because this exhibition exposes her by surrendering her to an ungraspable individuality (she can no longer be possessed, strictly speaking), and therefore with the complicity of the man who is loving her at that moment, she abandons herself—this is how she symbolizes a sacrifice. . . ." Once again, Bataille reenacts his pious beginnings in the Church to portray an atheological ritual that is part of his mystical vision for humanity. Madame Edwarda's self-sacrifice does make her "anguished as if in a hole" (OC, III, 24). She is not at peace with herself about the prostitution of her body. The story is one that narrates her withdrawal from total communion and self-sacrifice by giving her a transcendental, divine identity that the narrator eventually accepts.

The attribution of Madame Edwarda's divine identity may have something to do with Bataille's plan for this story as part of a trilogy he entitled *Divinus Deus*.[16] Although the trilogy was never finished, Bataille's second story of the series, *Ma Mère*, was published posthumously in 1966. The story has many autobiographical similarities to Bataille's relationships with his father and mother and thus contains much material for psychoanalytical approaches to his literature. However, I will restrict my comments to the narrative and its provocative fiction. The story is about the sexual education of Pierre Angélique as a young man. Pierre and his father have a difficult relationship centering on the father's education of his son's sexuality; he leaves obscene photographs in his study for his son to examine. The father dies shortly thereafter, when the son is 17. The mother uses several prostitutes to educate her son sexually by seducing him. The son's way to access his manhood and life itself is to say goodbye to the father (and death) with an erection because, as Bataille remarks elsewhere: "A man cannot see a burial without having an erection to such an extent that he had to leave his father's burial ceremony" (OC, II, 287). The son leaves his father and eventually parties with the disguised mother as a way of ritualizing his manhood and turning his back on death as well as on his origins. In a final masquerade party and orgy involving Pierre and several prostitutes, the mother unmasks herself to reveal that she is one of the women who have seduced the young man.

Incest is the one act that allows the mother to educate Pierre about what religion has done to him. She says early in the narrative that "I could do the worst in front of you, and I would be pure in your eyes" (Bataille, *Mère,* 20). The son often refers to his mother's divine/diabolical presence in his life, so she continues Madame Edwarda's divine identity within the cloak of a mother. Pierre, who was pious until his father's death (1906), describes his mother thus: "In her crimes my mother was closer to God than anything I had seen in the [stained-glass] window of the Church" (Bataille, *Mère,* 40). The mask of the masquerade party allows the mother to diguise her maternity and reveal to her seduced son the final "oblique smile" (Bataille, *Mère,* 125) of the ultimate obscenity, incest. She is "divine" in her sacred, transcendent mother's power, which cannot be fathomed by her child.

Of course, this story presents yet another face to Bataille's story about himself and his relationships to his parents. While "Le Petit" suggests that Bataille's father molested him as a child, *Ma Mère* inverts the traditional Freudian triangle because "Here it is the mother who wants to 'kill' the father" (Lukacher, 168). Nevertheless, the sacred nature of parenthood is called into question by Bataille's narratives and given a diabolical twist. Once again, the narrator's parents express the alliance of sexuality with death, a continuing obsession for Bataille throughout his work. The French expression **ce petit mort** (OC, III, 150), "the endearing dead one," for orgasm fascinates Bataille as if to say that the contrast of the expiated energy of sexual excitement followed by the quiet acceptance of what is other than excitement prepares him for the ultimate confrontation with his own death. Lucette Finas (175) dares another interpretation derived from *Madame Edwarda*: "This is a maternal gesture. Is Bataille impotent? Childhood, infirmity, and cramps constitute the system of Bataille the scribe." Why is the narrating voice maternal? The mother's sexuality passes through him. His concerns about sexual provocation, especially by his parents, could also be concerns about his own death, his own sexual impotence resulting from his fears about inheriting his father's syphilis.

Bataille's literary fragments help his readers to study the psychoanalytical implications of his obsessions. For example, Bataille planned a trilogy called *Divinus Deus* in which the three volumes would be *Madame Edwarda*, *Ma Mère*, and an unfinished work called *Charlotte d'Ingerville*. This projected third novel is once again narrated by Pierre Angélique, who at 16 years old is continuing the narrative of his sexual education, this time with Charlotte, who is 21 years old. Charlotte, the older woman who is not so old, is a friend of the family and an acquaintance of Pierre's mother. From her perspective outside the family, she bears witness to Pierre's mother's sexuality: "When I see God, it is in the form of the passion which is burning in your mother's heart and which nothing could squelch" (OC, IV, 285). Divinity, sexuality, and maternity are sources of energy and inspiration for the narrator's desire. Through his mother, this sexual energy, which is mystical and yet materialistic, is alive in him as he ponders his sexual relationship with the dying Charlotte.

The fourth volume of Bataille's collected works contains miscellaneous fictional narratives worth reading for their insights into Bataille's vision. "Julie," a story about a trio of two women and a man, is noteworthy for its fascination with nakedness and the appearance of Julie, after locking herself in her room, "at the door opening on the impossible" (OC, IV, 103). Regarding the issue of nakedness for Bataille, Michael Richardson (*Bataille,* 38) explains it well: "When we are naked we are faced with the anguish of our origins and our incompleteness; naked, we contemplate an inadequacy at the heart of ourselves." With *Le Mort*, which was published posthumously in 1967, Bataille's necrophilia returns in a vivid, literal association of the death of a beloved Edouard with the sexual orgies of Marie. The abyss of anguish before the presence of death returns in several other narratives ("La Maison Brûlée"; "La Tombe de Louis XXX"; "Louise Laroche"; "La Déesse et la Noce"; "La Houpette") contained in Bataille's collected works. These are either far short of being novels, or they are unfinished for one reason or another. The novels themselves are the more provocative commentaries because of their sustained and developed visions. Bataille's novels sometimes elicit a reaction from readers like that of Shadia Drury (122): "His novels often read like scripts of grade B horror films. The latter try to terrify their audience, but elicit laughter instead." However, Bataille may have been trying to do both with his fiction. Certainly, he is opposed to usefulness, which his literary ventures undermine. As Bataille himself once said to René Char, "Whether the writer wants to or not, the spirit of literature always sides with squandering, with the absence of definite goals, and with passion whose only purpose is to eat away at itself, to play the part of gnawing remorse . . . opposite the path of utility."[17] And Bataille's poetry went even further along that opposing path.

## Haunting Poetry

Bataille's poetry has a haunting quality. His work *Impossible* was at first entitled *Haine de la poésie*, that is, the hatred of poetry. However, Bataille's very style is poetic in that he often writes in an allusive and mystical way, not overly concerned with literal sense. He admired the surrealist program and defines it as "the truly virile opposition (nothing conciliatory or divine) of admitted limits and a rigorous will not to be submissive" (OC, XI, 31). "Virile" appears to limit this struggle for intellectual independence as a sexist appropriation of essence of manhood. We should qualify this insight by noting once again that the word *viril* was used by many advocates of action (e.g., André Malraux, Drieu la Rochelle) during the 1930s and 1940s. Instead, we should today understand that for Bataille virile meant the essence of humanity. Bataille did include women in this vision. His crucial role in having

Colette Peignot's poetry published is a case in point.[18] Indeed, her poetry is often erotic, as she explains in a letter to Bataille: "The poetic work is sacred in that it is the creation of a topical event, 'communication' reexperienced as *nudity.* It is the rape of the self, making naked, the communication to others of what is the reason for living, but this very reason for living is 'displaced' " (Laure, 89). Bataille's poetry is sometimes narrated from a woman's perspective in orgasm (OC, IV, 11–29) to express the eroticism of her pleasure. In contrast to Breton in *Nadja* (1928), where a woman is idealized and made into an abstract muse, Bataille's women are usually grounded in their materialistic bodies with all their problems and pleasures. One could perhaps object to Bataille's male appropriation of a woman's voice. He at least, however, made the effort to speak from the other side. Given his dispute with Breton, Bataille's poetic style is not simply the surrealist technique of reproducing a dreamworld. Fantasies are grounded in the details of base materialism. Although he is often mistakenly identified as a surrealist writer in manuals on literature, reading his poetry causes one to distinguish his style as distant from Breton's idealism. For example, in "Le Séminaire" ("The Seminary"), one reads the erotic woman's voice inviting ("I spread my legs open for the bull's tongue / in my beaver" [OC, IV, 29]) and enjoying a heterosexual enounter ("A long prick was spewing in the chapel of my heart" [OC, IV, 29]). Having been allied and then disenfranchised by Breton from surrealism, Bataille sought his own style independent of Breton's shamanistic control of what "automatic writing" meant.

Poetically, Bataille was significantly influenced by Jules Monnerot, whose *La Poésie moderne et le sacré* appeared in 1945. Note the alliance of the sacred with poetry. Bataille, having been intrigued by the sacred throughout his writings, finds another avenue for the expression of his reflections. Monnerot exalts the role of a shaman and magic in poetry and castigates the promotion of poetic technique, which he sees as an oxymoron (Monnerot, 28). Bataille assumed the role of the shaman in many of his intellectual ventures. So he himself explores magical associations in poetry. For example, in his *L'Archangélique*, he links a slaughterhouse with a church to visualize his image of his anxiety: "[I]n the face of the wall of anguish / the dark night is a church / where a pig is being butchered" (OC, III, 89). The sacrifice of the lowly pig in the church unites the theoretically higher-order concerns of religion with the theoretically lower-order sacrifice of pork. This is the nexus of Bataille's base materialistic vision in which pure violence has sovereign interest in that it focuses human concerns in the context of the here and now. Artificial hierarchies, with abstract distinctions between high and low positions, do not govern the universe. Nor are there any laws to frame human anxiety about the doubts of human power and its shortcomings. Bataille therefore sees the power of poetic thinking in the recognition that "true poetry is outside of laws" (OC, III, 218). This appears to bring him back to surrealism, especially Breton's version, which insists on being socially outrageous as well as religiously concerned (with Breton as its "Pope," of course). Although Bataille's poetic writings are on the margins of surrealism officially, he himself admitted in an interview with Madeleine Chapsal (*Envoyez,* 235) that "Surrealism appears to me to go to the heart of the matter." He did not speculate then what that meant. However, one can decide that because his own poetry is concerned with the nature of the sacred and its expression through base materialism that surrealism inspired him to experiment with similar problems in different ways.

As a practicing poet, Bataille has insights into the art of writing, and, hence, the links between literature and the arts. He is intrigued by the visual nature of painting. In his lecture "The Sorcerer's Apprentice" (1937) for the *Collège de Sociologie,* Bataille expresses his vision that "Art and literature express something that does not seem to run around with its head cut off like erudite laws" (Hollier, *College,* 15). This headless aberration of laws is a strange metaphor because of Bataille's experiments with sovereignty and the acephalic deities. The presence and control of art and literature, however, are also complementary as Bataille admits that "language is inadequate because it is composed from propositions that interject identities . . ." (OC, VI, 350). Clearly, Bataille is uncomfortable with language as the sole form of communication. What paintings offer are access to myth: "But when art recognizes the ultimate reality and the superior nature of the real world which contains humanity, myth enters into human existence like a force necessitating that the *inferior* reality be submissive to its realm" (OC, I, 536). Van Gogh and Manet attract Bataille because of their portrayal of light, especially the sun (OC, II, 418), which Bataille himself depicts in his narratives as the economic model for limitless self-generating energy. This tendency toward visual representation is part of Bataille's poetic vision that he develops through his art criticism.

Bataille is attracted by Van Gogh's tendency toward self-immolation and how the sun influences this tendency. This recalls for Bataille the Aztec sacrifices to the sun-god and the classical Greek model of Icarus. For him, there is clearly a metaphoric chain in these stories that is part of his mystical vision: "How can we miss seeing the formation of a series of knots which rejoins so assuredly the ear, the asylum, the sun, the most striking of celebrations, and death" (OC, I, 499). Bataille studies painting for its poetic expression of primitive and originary relationships with communication. His book on Manet, who visualizes the sun in contrast with the base materials of dust and dirt,[19] and his portrayal of the sensuality of the Lascaux drawings, which express "the poetic animality of the caves" (OC, XII, 273), are his only books to be translated into English and published in the United States during his lifetime. Hence, Bataille first appears in this country as a visual and visionary writer, which is in keeping with his mystical sense of the universal applicability of his general economy.

Bataille would have painting participate with sculpture, dance, and music in what he calls "symbolic expense" (OC, I, 307). This once again is part of his refusal of utility as the guiding principle in economics. Hence, the paintings discovered in the Lascaux caverns of France on 12 September 1940 exemplify for him a basic premise about humanity: "Finally, it is not the work, but the play, which decided when the work of art was realized and when work became in turn, in authentic works of art, only a response to the concern for utility. Certainly humanity is essentially the animal who works" (OC, X, 594). Likewise, Bataille himself works at writing, which was turned into authentic works of art when the human spirit was ready to listen, that is, when what he writes becomes useful to humanity's sense of self. His essays reflect this sense of work and play more than any other part of his opus.

## The Work and Play of the Essayist

While Bataille often claimed not to be a serious philosopher (Surya, 412), his essays reveal this claim as a playful gesture that goes against the effects of his written work as an essayist. It is especially apparent in *La Part maudite* that Bataille has a philosophical bent regarding major issues.[20] I discuss five of these philosophical topics as crucial in his essay-writing. These five—eroticism, mysticism, ecstasy, the sacred, and primitive religion—provide the philosophical parameters for his skills as an essayist at play and at work. Appropriately, one of his proposals for a seminar group is called *Collège d'Études Socratiques* (OC, VI, 284), which is based on the Socratic dictum of "know thyself" and also on Bataille's own principle of nonknowledge ("the only thing I know is that I know nothing"). Between these two principles, Bataille works through philosophical play as if in a Socratic dialogue in which no definitive answer is ever given but that the work is in the play of discussion.

## The Expense of Eroticism

Given his predilection for how humanity expresses its sovereignty, Bataille's foray into the Catholic taboo of eroticism is an opportunity to bring together many of his readings and the experiences of his life, especially from his pious period. In *Dianus*, Monsieur Alpha has an illuminating question: "Isn't it the key to human nature that Christianity, having surpassed the necessary limits of life, in the sense that fear places them too close, is at the source of anguished eroticism, of all erotic infinity?" (OC, III, 172). Bataille does not answer Monsieur Alpha.

Bataille's essays on eroticism are collected as the second volume of *La Part maudite* with *Sur Nietzsche* the third volume. This position, between Bataille's reflections on the economy of expenditure and those on the developments of Nietzsche's challenges to go beyond the herd instincts of morality, is crucial. The economy of expenditure is understood in Bataille's portrayal of eroticism as the need to get beyond restrictions without eliminating them, to express human vital energy, what Bataille would express as the principle of human sovereignty. He learned this from Nietzsche but also from Sade, who taught him about "the relationship between death and sexual excitement" (OC, X, 17). Maurice Blanchot, who became a good friend of Bataille during World War II, also knew his Sade well. Together, they shared many a reflection on the nature of Sadean eroticism. Eroticism for Bataille is an avenue of access into the playfulness of human sovereignty and the abyss, an image crucial to Bataille's literary art of death and anxiety. Bataille's essays about the nature of eroticism reflect his work on Nietzsche and Sade. The abyss is his contribution to their discussions of sovereignty. Not only is eroticism a manifestation of human sovereignty from various types of repression for Bataille, but eroticism is also "treachery" (OC, X, 170) to that sovereignty as an expression of human anxiety. This treachery places an ambivalence at the heart of eroticism, an ambivalence that is related to the question of obscenity. As we have seen, Bataille experiments with obscenity in some of his fiction and poetry. Scatology, especially as it relates to the double meaning of *sacer* etymologically as "tainted" and "holy," participates in what Bataille calls "an obscenity which can make a person sexually excited [and] can also make another laugh" (OC, II, 71). Thus, the two orders of play and work are continually at stake within eroticism.

## The Inner Experiment

Bataille learns from Hindu Tantrism that a mystical crisis is provoked by sexual excitement. Hence, eroticism is also "an aspect of *inner life,* so to speak, of the religious life of humanity" (OC, XII, 397). Bataille finds the mystical writings of St. Teresa and St. John of the Cross to be too reliant upon the presence and absence of God. Instead, from his experience with the yoga of Hinduism, he prefers an experience such that "when going to the end means at least this: that the limit of knowledge as the end is transgressed" (OC, V, 20). He finds the word "mysticism" too confusing because ecstasy, ravishment, and meditated emotion are all implied in the same word. He prefers the term "inner experiment," which refers to a subjective reflection on the common bond of being with others, a search for community. For Bataille, this "inner experiment" is founded in sexual excitement. He clearly experiences this as a male: "In the first days when I meditated . . . I suddenly felt as if I were an erect penis" (OC, IV, 165). He presents the focus of the experience on a scale with that of eroticism: "The erotic moment is also the most intense (except for the experiment of the mystics). Hence it is placed at the summit of the human spirit" (OC, X, 268). Eroticism's position at the summit of human experience is challenged by what was formerly known as mysticism. Bataille changes the focus of attention from God to the impossible. Herein lies his challenge to humankind's obsession with the utility of human communication.

Bataille's reflections on the impossible provide a hint of a possible joy in the face of death. More than "a tacit challenge to the authority of traditional theology" that mysticism itself provides (Richman, 1982, 107), the impossible is a substitute focus for a transcendent God. In effect, this experiment with the impossible provides a type of drug for Bataille to keep away the thought of "the unbreathable emptiness" (OC, V, 10) that haunts him. Ernst Jünger once suggested to Bataille that "there exists an equivalence among *war, ritual sacrifice,* and *the mystical life*" (OC, VII, 251). Bataille interprets this to mean that "There is the same game of 'ecstasies' and 'terrors' wherein humanity is enmeshed in the games of heaven" (OC, VII, 251). Pushing the limits of what humanity can do effectively translates the sexual into the symbolic, the physical limitations of humanity into conceptual ones. Bataille wants to have access to what is yet to be achieved as he experiments with "the anguish of the secret" (OC, V, 29). For this reason, his experiment must lead him to a sense of ecstasy in the face of death. This joy is, for Bataille, "the only path with intellectual integrity that the search for ecstasy can follow" (OC, I, 554). This path leads him to what he calls "nonknowledge."

## The Promise of Ecstasy

In writing about ecstasy, Bataille distinguishes the ecstatic experience from a philosophical one. This method is not dialectical but epistemological. He insists that "a philosopher worthy of the name must be able to develop a line of thinking indefinitely, but I am incapable of following mine for a long time" (Chapsal, 234). He experiences a loss of control whereby ecstasy is set off against philosophy in exposing what he calls "nonknowledge." The negative expression of this experience is directly imitative of Hegel's second stage of the dialectic, without proceeding to Hegel's synthesis or the teleological model for the dialectic. The negation leading up to ecstasy is a refusal of the positive epistemological precedence of some mystics who focus on God. Instead, from the Hindu practice of yoga, Bataille adapts the attitude that "nonknowledge communicates ecstasy" in that "at its very inception nonknowledge is anguish" (OC, V, 66). This is the anguish one reads in Bataille's fiction and poetry, a discomfort with one's place in life. Ecstasy provides an experience defined, in the spirit of Bataille, by Jean-Luc Nancy as "the ontological as well as the epistemological impossibility of an absolute immanence."[21] Instead, ecstasy provides a type of release from the self's lack of place. Often, beginning in the anxious drives of desire, especially sexual ones, the self is lost in the abyss of anguish, as Bataille's characters in his novels and poetry experience. From the Hindus Bataille learns that "the Tantrics use sexual pleasure not to lose themselves in it but as a kind of springboard" (OC, V, 30). And so Bataille finds in ecstasy that kind of projection upward that he admires in Nietzsche's advocacy of human sovereignty: "Nietzsche's leap is the inner experiment, the ecstasy when the eternal return and Zarathustra's laughter are revealed" (OC, VI, 313). This leap is one that is out of time, that suggests Heidegger's *Ekstase,* the phenomenon "of the future, the character of having been."[22] Bataille adds that time is not so crucial because the experience is not an epistemological one. For example, Pierre, a character in the narrative fragment "Sainte," says to Sainte after their tryst: "I would not want you to know if we slept together last night" (OC, IV, 305). The experience of nonknowledge, in this case sexual pleasure, is already a communal act that subverts the anxiety of knowledge, the need to know.

Ecstasy, however, also means being in the world for Bataille because his sense of belonging, of having a place, is related to his being able to constantly challenge the limits of what "world" means. He asks: "At what level is my place? I have never counted while climbing the levels to get to myself; where all the levels end, there is my ceiling and my place" (OC, VI, 213). How to get there? This place is a type of utopia, literally "no place" in which one experiences the pleasures of laughing and sensuality in interaction with others. He finds that "in much the same manner as yawning is contagious, so is ecstasy" (Chapsal, 237). This contagion has to do with a human participation in this common experience, which is "common" not in its participation by many but in its universal availability. Bataille is so convinced by this that he claims that "Life . . . only achieves greatness and reality in ecstasy and in ecstatic love" (OC, I, 443). The communication that occurs in this experience is the basis for an interest that Bataille pursues throughout his writings on the sacred. We have already seen how his fiction and poetry explore this topic. His essays likewise discuss the nature of the sacred, that word whose etymology is derived from *sacer*, which also means sullied or base. The word *sacer* (OC, II, 62) inspires Bataille to explore heterology (**l'hétérologie**), the study of ambivalence at the core of the problems of identity. His base materialism is derived from the other side of the respectful and untouchable taboo ascribed by deistic cultures to what is determined to be sacred.

## Violence and the Sacred

The ritual of sacrifice intrigues Bataille with its appeal to the double meaning of *sacer*. On the one hand, he has a sociological interest learned from Durkheim about the sacred as a bond uniting a group of people by their respect for what is holy. The erotic mysticism and ecstasy promoted by Bataille participate in this godless bond with the sacred. On the other hand, there is the materialistic and gruesome side of the holy whereby death itself participates in the ritualization of a common practice by a group. Bataille readily links death and the sacred because "the slipping away outside the self in the face of death requires a sacred world so that when one is lost, some larger reality comes into view with ways to accommodate terror" (OC, II, 246). The group ritual involving the death of a living member of the group often entails violence, which is gruesome and usually involves suffering by the selected individual being sacrificed. Studying the ancient Greek, Roman, and Aztec sacrifices and still haunted by Borel's psychoanalysis involving the "100 forms of punishment," Bataille focuses on ritualized violence and respects the art of Goya, who has represented violence and terror, in Bataille's perspective, "as an art of excess, an art that recalls the violence of the sacred."[23] This insight into the "violence of the sacred" also kept Bataille enthralled by anthropological studies of ancient religions.

Although Bataille was first known in the United States for his views on the Lascaux cave sketches, he investigated many instances of how history explained violence and its excesses. For example, in 1959, he published his essays on the fifteenth-century character Gilles de Raies, popularly known in Nantes, Brittany, as the basis for the legend of Barbe-Bleu (Bluebeard). Gilles had been hanged and burned because of his reputed love of blood at the expense of many children. Bataille asks whether this case exemplifies that "history might be measured by the legend which alone has the power of evoking what, in crime, is not reducible to the limits of a known world" (OC, X, 282–83). Gilles might have been convicted based on conjecture about what happened and about the types of violence that he committed. Violence itself pushes the limits of what is acceptable according to the norms of a historical moment. History is thus a factor in the contextual understanding of the role of violence. Bataille challenges this limited understanding of violence with his ability to bring the sacred and violence into his own dimension whereby "I fix a point in front of me and represent this point to myself as the geometrical location of all existence" (OC, I, 556). To see himself and the location of himself as an other enables him to see death, the sacred, and violence all immutably linked in a secular vision of religion. In "Dianus," at the death of the brother of his mistress (E.), Monsieur Alpha violently steals into E.'s home for a look at the dead body and speaks with a voice very close to Bataille's own in his essays: "I cannot even doubt that, without the unacknowledgeable intrusion into E.'s home, I would not have been so delighted to be near the dead man; the bedroom, all in flowers, was like a church, and what penetrated with the long knife of ecstasy, wasn't the eternal light but the intolerable, empty smile of my brother" (OC, III, 172). First of all, the violence of the secret, forbidden entry into a sacred place provides the speaker with a rush of delight. Compounding this delight is an example in this scene of Bataille's notion that "nothing is sacred which wasn't once particular (although it now ceases to be so)" (OC, V, 271). This is no abstract pursuit of universal ideals. Rather, the sacred is grounded in individual experiences such as Monsieur Alpha's mistress and her dead brother. Finally, laughter enables another violence by exemplifying a break from the actual moment, a separation that the smile acknowledges.

The subtitle to Bataille's *Le Coupable* (begun in 1939), *La Divinité du Rire* ("The Divinity of Laughter"), expresses the alterity or otherness of one who laughs and also the altarity or sacrificial nature of being different to the point of martyrdom to life. This martyrdom is sacrificial in its token reminder of the ultimate reality of death toward which our lives are relentlessly drawn, as toward the emptiness, or **vide,** of E.'s dead brother as seen by Monsieur Alpha. From Durkheim, Bataille learns that "the equation religion = (sacrifice + wound)"[24] provides the foundation for mysticism in his sense of ecstasy. Hence the violence of the wound, which is not the destruction of war so present to Bataille when he was writing "Le Coupable," has a necessary affirmation in the promise and light of human freedom. As apparent in much of Bataille's work, the guilt of humanity is in taking responsibility for the violence toward a God who was invented in a confused attitude, as Bataille tells it: "Since God is only the confusion of the *sacred* (of the religious) and *reason* (of the useful), God only has a place in a world where the confusion of the useful and the sacred becomes the basis for a reassuring stance" (OC, V, 240). Instead, Bataille is interested in those rituals that preclude usefulness and certitude and yet reflect respect for the sacred.

## Toward a Cultural Humanism

Bataille has many essays on what appears to be either an anthropological or a sociological stance on primitive religions. His interests, nonetheless, are not merely anthropological or sociological. Rather, he is a humanist who seeks to understand the cultural ties that bring humans together. He examines the myths or stories that communities tell to explain themselves and their origins. These myths are sometimes legends confused by a community's need to give itself an identity, for example, the Bluebeard fantasy and the history of Gilles de Raies and Nantes, Brittany. Sometimes the myths are narrated through rituals that survive the original event. Bataille remarks that "a community which does not accomplish the ritual reenactment of its myths only possesses a declining truth" (OC, I, 535) about itself. The rituals interest Bataille as the means to convey a nonutilitarian version of a myth, as in the Lascaux drawings, where he observes "the useless representation of signs which seduce, which are born from emotions and are directed toward them" (OC, IX, 13). The animals depicted on the walls of the caves interact with humanity in a manner similar to the one implied in the Aztec rituals whereby the animal nature of humanity is destroyed and death is affirmed as being present within human life. The copresence of life and death is perhaps the most revealing principle that Bataille sees reaffirmed in the ritual narratives of a community's myths. The taboos placed on death, sexuality, and behavior outside a community's control become manifest in these rituals, which are usually not institutionalized practices. Often, they are group efforts that offer commentaries on the larger community to which the group belongs. Sometimes, it is the art of individuals who have repressed the community's taboos and then express a subversion or a transcendence of the taboos in art. The Lascaux drawings, for example, reveal that the animal component of human nature is not universally accepted. In fact, the opposite is sometimes reaffirmed, as Bataille notes: "What recalls the subsisting animality in us is the object of horror and elicits a reaction analogous to that produced by the forbidden" (OC, IX, 63). Hence, when art combines the features of humans and animals, Bataille is attracted to learn what this combination tells us about what a culture is hiding in its taboos.

Bataille's study of eroticism (*L'Érotisme*, 1957) appears, at first glance, to be sociological. He adapts Durkheim's theories with psychological and cultural insights that go beyond sociology. Bataille is especially astute in affirming the attractiveness of the forbidden, the forbidden in the very act of transgressing it, and the bond between the forbidden (**l'interdit**) and the need for a culture to identify itself while providing the parameters for going beyond itself. There does not even have to be a conscious will to transgress a taboo because, as Bataille says, "In principle the erotic experience commits us to silence" (OC, X, 186). Humanity is affirmed in the privacy of the erotic experience where words and direct rebellion are not necessary. In eroticism, Bataille exposes humanity's "inner religion" (OC, X, 36), which by its very nature is "treason" (OC, X, 168) to the community. In eroticism, he also finds a culture of sovereignty whereby humanity can express its freedom from the limitations of taboos and the utilitarian attitude toward reproduction. In the experience of eroticism, he differentiates women from men and finds women to be ideals of human communication in their eroticism: "Therefore women appear to be essentially dedicated to *communication,* understood in the strong sense of the word as the meaning of effusion: they must logically be objects of generosity from the members of their family who raise them" (OC, X, 205). This insight assumes women to be an other from a man's perspective. Bataille does show the socializing influence on gender and also his perspective as a male receiving the generosity of heterosexually oriented women. This is a naive reduction of women's eroticism that I discuss further in chapter 5.

Bataille also explores the cultural practices of gift giving that have affected women's fate. He is aware of Marcel Mauss's "Essay on the Gift" discussing potlatch customs as well as Claude Lévi-Strauss's insight into the incest taboo as a subtle mechanism to govern the exchange of women. While this latter theory exposes women as property to be bartered, Bataille does not acknowledge this reduction of women's humanity, which Simone de Beauvoir developed at length in her review of Lévi-Strauss's *Structures élémentaires de la parenté* (1949). Instead, Bataille sees the practice as an act based upon generosity (OC, X, 207, n. 1). Although his vision of human generosity may be ethically admirable, his blindness to the inhumanity of women in this practice must be faulted. This ethical concern with generosity is also discussed at length in chapter 5.

The practices of gift giving are a recurrent concern in Bataille's essays. For him, the cultural phenomenon of potlatch, a ceremonial feast among some Native American communities in which gifts are distributed, is linked to provocation (OC, I, 311) and religious sacrifice (OC, I, 281) in their social context. Once again, the sociological insights are not the final product for Bataille. The individual's existential status regarding others within a cultural milieu interests Bataille even more than the survival of either the society or the anthropological stakes of gift giving. From Mauss, Bataille learns that "the lesson of potlatch lies in the fundamentally ambivalent nature of the things exchanged" (Richman, *Reading,* 62). As gifts change the status quo of relationships by introducing a new element between individuals, these gifts can provoke others into obligation and/or anger toward the giver. Bataille has a similar fascination with the phenomenon of amuck in the Malaysian Islands, whereby in a religious frenzy one struck randomly with a knife the first passerby in the tribal community, recalling the surrealist passion in the early 1920s of firing a pistol into a crowd. For Bataille, amuck, like gifts, is an example of the crisis of violence that expresses a suicidal urge to sacrifice an unknown member of the community in order to change the individual's anxiety about life within the community. Similarly, Bataille not only wrote many essays, whose titles in addition to those I have reviewed here are listed in the table of contents at the rear of his collected works, he was also anxious about directing the intellectual scope of various communities and consequently was active in founding and editing journals during his career. Let us look at the nature of this type of literary involvement to see why it attracted him.

## The Face of the Editor

Bataille was astute in realizing that his fate was governed by political circumstances. He became involved in the politics of his moment. In his youth, he proposed to Michel Leiris the avant-garde group *Oui* as an alternative to the nihilism of the dadaists. He was attracted by surrealism and contributed a translation in 1925 to the surrealist journal *La Révolution surréaliste*. This was the beginning of his interest in groups formed for intellectual purposes and in journals that published the work of those groups.

Bataille became fascinated with journals and how they often spawned an intellectual cohort. With his colleague Pierre d'Espézal from the Bibliothèque Nationale, who was the editor of the journal *Aréthuse* and who convinced the art collector Georges Wildenstein to provide funding for a new journal in 1929, Bataille became general secretary for the journal *Documents,* which was dedicated to art and ethnography and published under the auspices of the Musée du Trocadéro. Bataille worked closely with Georges-Henri Rivière, the director of the museum, to produce the first issues of the journal. It is only in the fourth issue that Bataille's anti-idealistic influence can be seen with his contribution of articles on the Aztecs and their rituals of death and sacrifice. The journal is especially marked by photographs and visual displays that Bataille learned from the surrealists. This tendency to combine the visual with words is an eidetic feature of much of Bataille's own writing. Michael Richardson describes the effect of such "incongruous juxtaposition" in *Documents* of printed matter and visual images as achieving "a sort of dialectic between word and image which served to emphasize how much representation served to distort the nature of the phenomenon which it represented" (Richardson, *Bataille,* 51). Bataille's lifelong passion for painting and the visual arts probes this opposition and eventually subverts it with the affirmation of the human anxiety about communication. He is continually intrigued with the painter's plight of being "condemned to please" (OC, XI, 480) with a tableau. He is often struck, as with some of Goya's and Manet's works, by "a definitive silence" (OC, IX, 132) that paintings exude. However, in the journal *Documents*, there is still the ethnological interest in the visual as a type of grounding in truth. Bataille's mark is to question that truth with a materialism that directly opposes André Breton's dedication of surrealism to the *merveilleux* ("the awesome"). In the two years and 15 issues of *Documents*, not once did Bataille cite Breton. It was in 1930, midway during Bataille's tenure with *Documents*, that Bataille and 11 other erstwhile colleagues of Breton published the pamphlet *Un Cadavre* mocking Breton's program for surrealism.

In *Documents*, Bataille saw himself as providing an alternative to Breton's purported idealism. For example, in the dictionary provided for the journal, he writes the entry for the word *informe* without ever defining it. Instead, as Rosalind Kraus has developed, Bataille opposes the term to "the abstractness of concepts and the prissiness with which they are meant to contain."[25] He proposed a base materialism that could transgress without transcending and produce formlessness. Nevertheless, in 1931, Wildenstein withdrew his financial support apparently because *Documents* was not selling well. Although the journal had a short life, it remains a representative of a climate in which surrealism was making an ideological claim on the French avant-garde. André Masson, the surrealist painter and associate of Bataille at the time, claims that the originality of *Documents* was entirely due to Bataille.[26]

Meanwhile, Bataille began affiliations with several other journals that had political ties. By 1931, Bataille already contributed to the anti-Stalinist journal *La Critique sociale*. He had joined the group *Cercle Communiste Démocratique* in 1930. The founder, Boris Souvarine, directed the journal to which Bataille would contribute until 1934. Bataille and his group of colleagues played a major role during the early 1930s in helping Souvarine direct *La Critique sociale*. Bataille published his essays on expenditure in this journal. During the period of 1932 to 1933, he also became one of the founders of the surrealist journal *Minotaure,* whose title he proposed.

Bataille's work with journals during the 1930s was marked by a period of intense commitment to group politics. The journals were a means to disseminate ideas collectively, to make contacts with leading intellectuals, and to begin having an influence on others. Concomitant with his association with journals, Bataille organized socialist seminars called *Masses* with René Lefebvre (1933) and a surrealist antifascist political activist group with Roger Caillois called *Contre-Attaque* (1935), which produced one issue of its publication entitled *Cahiers de Contre-*

*Attaque*. Colette Peignot (Laure), whom he had met during his affiliation with *La Critique sociale*, joined him in many of these political ventures. The common thread in all of his politics was the rejection of the values of the bourgeois world. During 1935, he even flirted with fascism because of its espousal of violence as an extreme option in a world fraught with confusion about the onset of war.

In 1935, Bataille also founded the journal *Acéphale*. This was the predecessor to the secret society of the same name that he would organize in 1937. The journal, whose title referred to the headless deity of chthonic origins whom Bataille asked André Masson to sketch, was dedicated to the work of Nietzsche, whose work Bataille had studied with Leon Chestov. During the period from 1936 to 1939, the only four issues of *Acéphale* appeared. By focusing on Nietzsche and his principles of sovereignty, this journal gave Bataille the opportunity to attract parties interested in provocation and to organize his secret society. The presence of Colette Peignot (Laure) in the group, and, later, Isabelle Waldberg, is a commentary on Bataille's nonexclusionary attitude toward women. Some of his readers think that his sexist attitudes tend to make women disappear.[27] I would argue that his attitude toward women was governed by the individual women in question. For example, both Colette Peignot and Isabelle Waldberg were women with intellectual status. They had something to say and would not allow themselves to be reduced to a vacuum and thus fought for their place in Bataille's coterie.

Bataille also made some attempts to marshal the research in psychology. Bataille had been psychoanalyzed by Adrien Borel in 1927. In the spring of 1937, Bataille participated in a symposium on circumcision, during which he learned that several participants were interested in meeting regularly. In 1938, Bataille brought his psychoanalyst Adrien Borel together with René Allendy, Pierre Janet, Michel Leiris, and Paul Schiff into the *Société de psychologie collective.* They met monthly during 1938 and 1939 to hear papers on topics of interest. Bataille gave the introductory lecture on attitudes toward death. Bataille's involvement with this group demonstrated his continued interest in the politics of his intellectual influence. In this society, he was the vice president, and the president was Pierre Janet, the well-known professor.

The war brought a strange lull to Bataille's drive to control intellectual collectives. Although he continued to write during the war and established ties with Maurice Blanchot, he did not appear to engage in any collective ventures until the end of the war. His writings (especially

"Le Coupable") indicate a severe depression. During this period, his writings may have been a type of therapy for his inability to exert the intellectual influence in groups that he had previously manifested. Nevertheless, his discussions with Blanchot proved so fruitful that he founded in 1946 in Vézelay the journal *Critique*, which would not be restricted to the chauvinism that had marked the previous decade. Instead, the journal was oriented toward books both in and out of France that were deemed to have certain intellectual influence. This was a bold move, no doubt inspired by Blanchot's cosmopolitan intellectual attitude. The timing may not have been right, however. The mood in France was indeed chauvinistic. The Occupation, the Resistance, and de Gaulle were heading the French toward a provincialism that threatened the existence of *Critique*. Several times, Jérôme Lindon, the son of Laure and Bataille and the editor at Editions de Minuit in Paris, had to intervene and save the journal from extinction because of poor circulation.[28] Today the journal continues to be a major voice in Paris for the exchange of ideas between France and intellectuals from the rest of the world. The celebrity of the journal happened only after Bataille's death. Here again, Bataille's active editing and contributions to the journal were not well known during his lifetime. He did, however, make a place for himself in intellectual history through his responsibilities as an editor of journals. *Critique* remains as a continuing forum for the exchange of ideas that Bataille, along with Blanchot, envisioned. Let us now look at Bataille the politician, a role that belied many of his journal activities.

## In the Throes of Politics

Politics for Bataille is the struggle to achieve the impossible for a bourgeois society that respects utility and homogeneity. At first, this appears to be a Marxist agenda, as in the way Joseph Libertson presents Bataille's opponent as "the homogeneous society, or the homogeneous sector of a given society, . . . based on an adherence to the concept of utility as manifested in the process of production."[29] Bataille, however, was not limited to one ideological avenue. He was fascinated by the ideal of the so-called "man of action," like other writers of his generation such as André Malraux, Drieu la Rochelle, Paul Nizan, and Louis Aragon. Unlike them, however, he preferred a more abstract approach, what he calls "the politics of the impossible" (OC, III, 521). This approach is a simultaneous refusal to wait while the world unfolds and a revolt against strategies that present themselves as complete and self-sufficient. "The politics of the impossible" is a subversive attitude toward ideologies and is consistent with Bataille's view of human sovereignty.[30] Like his contemporaries, he is likely to use the adjective virile to describe how the man of action is responsible within the politics of the impossible. For Bataille, the man of action "remains virile only in seeking to make reality conform to what he thinks" (Hollier, *College,* 16). Thus, for Bataille, the intellectual finds meaning in politics, although he was never content and perhaps because he was never effective enough in working with others to have seen political reality conform to his thoughts. As he looked back on his political involvements during the late 1920s and the 1930s, he told Marguerite Duras in 1957 that "I was never involved in political life. What always mattered to me was to understand" (Duras, 212). This comment was probably directed at those who accuse him of flirting with fascism because of his published essays ("La Structure psychologique du fascisme," OC, I, 339–71; "Le fascisme en France," OC, II, 205–13; and "Essai de définition du fascisme," OC, II, 214–16). It must be remembered that these essays appeared in *La Critique sociale*, an anti-Stalinist communist journal. Bataille always took a political position against right-wing agencies, such as that of "royal power," whereby homogeneity would reign (OC, I, 358) rather than human sovereignty. He was obsessed with the need for political change, as was his hero of *Le Bleu du ciel,* who says: "Because I was driven by a happy insolence, I had to upset everything, by every means to upset everything" (OC, III, 455). Despite Bataille's words to the contrary, he too had a "happy insolence" that drove him into the throes of political struggles, even though these did not constitute his "life."

Bataille was especially opposed to capitalism and fascism as viable political agendas. The uses of violence by fascist groups, however, attracted Bataille as a means to awake bourgeois capitalist lethargy and to inspire action. For example, he speaks about discussing with Raymond Queneau, Jean Piel, and Simone Kahn the failures of the 1934 riots between the communists and the fascists and viewing this event as a "thwarted expectation" (OC, II, 262) for the situation of the workers on strike. The implication here is that Bataille had expectations that the violence could introduce a whole new series of realized political agendas. Nevertheless, by 1935, Bataille became involved by organizing with Roger Caillois the antifascist surrealist group called *Contre-Attaque,* which had communist leanings. Bataille wrote political pamphlets for this group, although none of them have been found to date.[31] The group managed to publish one issue of *Cahiers de Contre-Attaque* in May 1936, even though they had disbanded as a group in January of that year.

Bataille was resilient in finding political means to express his agitation. While the journal *Acéphale* was founded in 1935, Bataille and his comrades claimed to have acted "acephalically" in 1936 by spilling blood in the Place de la Concorde and placing a skull there in memory of Louis XVI. This act, committed in the spirit of human sovereignty, was later recollected when the secret society of *Acéphale* was founded by Bataille in 1937 with Colette Peignot and other comrades attracted to the chthonic cult of the headless god. Only eight members of the group are now known.[32] Their effect politically was quite restrained since the membership and their actions were clandestine. Some testimony as to what they did has been revealed since then so that we now know that the group worshiped the Acéphale god in an oak tree trunk, climbed the volcano of Mount Etna, and held secret meetings to discuss the writings of Nietzsche. Indeed, Bataille wrote in *Combat* in 1944 that there had to be a war mounted against the propaganda value of literature: "This war is waged against a life-style whose propaganda literature is the key. The fatalism of fascism is to enslave: among others to reduce literature to utility."[33] To counter the use of propaganda, not only with literature but also with rituals, the *Acéphale* group explored political alternatives to fascism's dominating program of utility. The *Acéphale* secret society was deemed to be political by Bataille because, as Alan Stoekl observes: "Bataille considered it a dangerous mistake to leave the monopoly of [the sacred]'s political exploitation to the fascists, the only ones so far to have recognized its importance."[34] Bataille's interest in the fascists is thus recognized to have effects not limited to political agendas but extending into his own concern with religion as a process of communication. The problem with the fascist model of religion, for Bataille, had to do with its promotion of the presence of God such that "God is the realization in his theological aspect of the supreme sovereign form" (OC, I, 361). This God was too alien from humanity for Bataille. He did, however, admire the political violence that many fascists practiced, despite their right-wing allegiances.

The violence of fascism was useful for Bataille in opposing both capitalism and Christianity in their political realities. Bataille preferred the human sovereignty of someone like Gilles de Raies, whom Shadia Drury (116) portrays for Bataille as "the holy sinner." Gilles de Raies is the incarnation of the political and historical implementation of transgression. Transgression, as Bataille develops in his *L'Erotisme*, is an affirmation of the needs for both the limitations on human behavior and their subversion as manifestations of human sovereignty. As Blanchot (*Entretien,* 308) appropriately observes, "The forbidden marks the point where power ends." Bataille makes the stakes between the political and the religious even clearer as he claims that to condemn transgression is to banish "the sacred from the world of religion or a profanation of religion itself."[35] Religion was a part of the politics he practiced. On the one end of the spectrum, he admires communism because it is "necessarily in agreement with the sovereignty of human life" (Duras, 20). On the other end he placed capitalism, whose utilitarian economics he opposed with his book *La Part maudite,* which he called "the condemnation of capitalism as the irrational style of life" (OC, II, 24, n.). After World War II, Bataille strongly indicated his preference for the Marshall Plan (OC, VII, 164), which called for cooperation among all the economic systems of the world to alleviate the feverish climate of war. He could see that this economic of expense would improve communication through communion, an attitude that his views of science supported.

## The Nonknowledge of the Sciences

The sciences of economics, anthropology, psychoanalysis, architecture, and numismatics also intrigued Bataille. His intellectual commitments to atheology, base materialism, and transgression oriented him toward surpassing taboos and discovering what is beyond the limits imposed on human knowledge. As we have already seen, Blaise Pascal, a seventeenth-century mathematician and intellectual who proffered the great wager about faith, appeals to Bataille with his reflections on the nature of risk: "Pascal . . . did not want to risk anything; he remained Christian; was this possibly virtuous?" (OC, VI, 245). The risk of nonknowledge haunts Bataille considerably more than it did Pascal. While Pascal began with the certainty of science and evolved intellectually toward the certainty of faith, Bataille begins with the certainty of faith, questions that certainty, and probes the alleged certainty of the sciences. Bataille is much more intrigued by the uncertainties of the abyss of nonknowledge with all its risks than by the promises of institutional religion and a transcendent God. For him, "The object of science is to found the homogeneity of phenomena . . . science cannot know *heterogeneous* elements in themselves" (OC, I, 344).

In the *Collège de Sociologie,* Bataille encountered the challenges of science in the person of Roger Caillois. Bataille, who describes Caillois as a "sociologist . . . basically limited by objectivity" (OC, XII, 51), appealed to Caillois's scientific pretensions in a letter of 21 August 1937: "Some of us should not at the very least contemplate a personal effort less great than that demanded by scientific movements" (Bataille, *Lettres,* 63). Bataille's love affair with science was not limited to sociology, as it was for Caillois. Indeed, Michèle Richman notes that "refusing the title of sociologist, Bataille preferred to identify himself as a sorcerer's apprentice" (Richman, *Collège,* 84). As a self-defined sorcerer's apprentice, Bataille was intrigued by the scientific lore of nonknowledge to which Bataille wants access in heterogeneous detail.

## Anthropology's Entry into Human Rituals

Human sacrifice and the mystical aura of eroticism held a special interest for Bataille in his readings and explorations of anthropological research. On the one hand, rather than what Bataille calls the Christian symbolic rituals of sacrifice ("Christians have only ever known symbolic sacrifice" [OC, X, 89]; of course this ignores the martyrdom of the early Christians), anthropology as a science exposes the cultural practices of human sacrifice to provide a living model of the sacred. This model juxtaposes the discontinuity of death with a ritual for the living who are manifesting their communal continuity (OC, X, 84). Likewise, with the sacrifice of animals, as in the prehistoric drawings in the Lascaux caverns where what appears is the sacrifice or hunt of animals, "The ancestors [of contemporary humanity] disguised their traits with the mask of the animal" (OC, XII, 277). On the other hand, anthropology discovers practices that are outside the autonomy of knowledge that the scientific method claims for itself (OC, I, 526). The tantric rituals of Hinduism, for example, suggest the provocation of mystical crises by sexual excitement (OC, X, 239). This is an area Bataille identifies with nonknowledge and that anthropological science often identifies with "the black magic [which] has continued this tradition until the present day" (OC, I, 224). Bataille prefers to look at this body of information, which he often calls "the holy" (**le sacré**), like the human body, which cultures often respect as "holy" except when it is a cadaver being autopsied on an operating table (OC, XII, 48). This preference has the effect of exploding that which is considered to be protected and saved for a restrictive utilitarian purpose by the sciences that claim knowledge as their property. Bataille's appreciation for Claude Lévi-Strauss's *Tristes Tropiques* (1955), an autobiographical and personalized account of the author's encounters with the native cultures in the Amazon basin of Brazil, is not surprising in this respect: "Enlightenment linked with non-knowledge at the very time when anguish and madness are linked to science demonstrates to us the virtue of this approach . . ." (OC, XII, 394). Science reveals the limitations of knowledge while nonknowledge reveals what lies beyond and beckons to be experienced. There is much more at stake with nonknowledge because its very identification leads Bataille to propose a generalized economy that does not respect the misleading criterion of utilitarian knowledge.

## Economics and Restrictive Knowledge

Bataille advocates a generalized economy whereby expense is the viable principle. He offers a generalized economy as the alternative to a science of economics that has advocated surpluses and savings for the utilitarian goals of accumulating profits with individualistic greed and ignores the potential of surplus to become explosive. The Aztec festivals provide examples for Bataille that surpluses are volatile in that "the victim is a surplus caught in the mass of useful wealth" (OC, VII, 64). Similarly, massacres, war, and large-scale violence have resulted throughout history as countries have amassed financial surpluses to create weapons of destruction aimed at imperial growth. Instead, Bataille offers the example of the sun with its continuous expense of energy: "The sunray that *we are* finally returns to nature and the sun's meaning; we must give ourselves, *lose ourselves without accountability*" (OC, VII, 10). Bataille proposes the general distribution of "the damned portion" (*La Part maudite*) of society's income, the "increase in wealth [which] is the largest that there ever was" (OC, VII, 44). He thus advocates a general economy that is not limited to a specific sector of society but rather is modeled upon the energy of the universe. Bataille returns to Mauss's study of the gift to recuperate the potlatch ritual of isolated societies as exhibiting the ideal of "consumption for others" ( OC, VII, 72). However, Bataille's concern with others does not resolve the issues of personal anxiety and the place of the self. For this, he delves into the rising science of psychoanalysis, for which he has had an abiding concern since his earliest writings.

## The Place of Anguish in Psychoanalysis

Bataille's earliest fiction bears witness to narrators and characters who are wracked with personal anguish about their sexual identity. He claims about himself that "anguish bears witness to my fear of communicating, of losing myself" (OC, V, 67). He was curious about the "science" of psychoanalysis and its supposed isolation of consciousness and the unconscious. In 1927, he submitted himself to psychoanalysis by Adrien Borel. The photographs Borel showed him of the "100 forms of punishment" remained etched in Bataille's memory: "I am haunted by the picture of the Chinese executioner in my photos working to cut off the victim's leg at the knee—the victim tied to the post with his eyes turned up, his head back, and the grimace of his lips allowing us to see his teeth" (OC, V, 275). The photographs exhibited the relationships between suffering as a mystical experience and the physical inducements of pain. In *L'Abbé C.*, Charles's psychotherapist oddly admits that "our science only has authority insofar as it doesn't humiliate the sick" (OC, III, 251). This reluctant interest of psychoanalysis to convey the whole truth reveals Bataille's own reservations about what the analyst may decide to keep hidden. After Bataille's psychoanalysis by Borel, he was able to begin writing again (after his pious writings). His struggles continued in his writings. Psychoanalysis made manifest his struggles with base materialism and death that he would later explore and develop through writing.

Psychoanalysis also guided Bataille into his interests in the sacred and human ritual. The mystical rites of physical pleasure and suffering caused him to reflect upon the relationships among the human, the animal, and the divine. He observes, for example, that "only animals have retained these supernatural qualities that humans have lost . . ." (OC, XII, 516). Hence, by focusing on humanity's physicality and base materialism through rituals of eroticism and his version of mysticism, humanity might recover that "sacredness" that had been generally ignored in favor of utilitarian concerns. In Bataille's "Theory of Religion," he focuses upon the interest of psychoanalysis toward self-consciousness in its interconnected implications with "self-consciousness directing toward intimacy the lamp that science elaborated to clarify objects" (OC, VII, 341). The positivist methods of general science offer a model for what religion can reveal about the self and its relationships to others. For example, the mask, a key element in such stories as *Ma Mère,* receives an extended comment in "le Catéchisme de Dianus": "What appears to be desirable is masked; the mask falls one day or another when what is unmasked is anguish, death, and the annihilation of the perishable being" (OC, V, 402). So the mask is necessary to disguise his insecurity because "the mask still retains the force of appearing on the threshold of this clear and reassuring world of anxiety as an indistinct incarnation of chaos" (OC, II, 403). Chaos and the brink of the abyss have also reappeared throughout his works that were ostensibly about other topics.

Bataille's concerns about sovereignty through the ages, and its reassertion by oppressed groups, are linked to his insights into the mask. His interest in the trials of Gilles de Raies is a case in point since the common people had invented a legend of the cruelty of this lord of the manor as if to justify his seigneurial power. Gilles de Raies himself legitimized his place among the myths of France: "No doubt, he made himself into a superstitious representation, as if he was made of another nature, a supernatural being in his own way, helped by God and the devil" (OC, X, 280). This legend of Bluebeard was created by the people who wanted to believe in the power of the cruel overclass and was contrasted to what Bataille calls "the tragedy of feudalism and the tragedy of nobility" (OC, X, 319), that is, the downfall of a system in which sovereign power was legitimized through belief in such a hierarchy of humanity.

Bataille comments that for himself "only impotence is cruel" (OC, III, 175). The word impotence is polyvalent for the self in political and sexual contexts. The personal sexual context may be especially pertinent to Bataille, whose father died from syphilis and whose writings are marked throughout with admiration for virility and sovereignty. Likewise, his concern with the *petit mort* or orgasmic pleasure combines impotence with the lack of power that comes with death: "Death is linked with tears, and sometimes sexual desire is also linked with laughter. But laughter is not as much as it seems to be in contrast to tears; the object of laughter and the object of crying always go together with some kind of violence, interrupting the usual course, the habitual course of things" (OC, X, 585). Thus Bataille is also interested that science accounts for the "normal" course of things, as interrupted by the self and its drive toward sovereignty.

## Architecture and Physics: The Power of Structure

Always curious about the abyss as a kind of structure that holds daunting power as an image of anxiety from both the inside and the outside of its experience, Bataille is attracted to the sciences of architecture and physics in their explanations of the principles of nature. Both sciences had revealed a structure for existence with which Bataille was uncomfortable. While the abyss is a romantic symbol of the awe that the yawning universe inspires in the beholder, it is also, for Bataille, an image of the human need for expense and excess. To go beyond the limits imposed either internally or externally implies understanding those limits, so Bataille studied the limits of nature as science presented them. Architecture (**l'architecture**) offers the limitations of stasis, the conditions of staying in one place, while physics studies the laws of motion, moving beyond one place.

On the one hand, nature sometimes appears to imitate the human tendency to inhabit one place. Perhaps the anthropomorphic tendencies of sciences portray nature in this way, as does Bataille with his description of the flowers in a field "which sometimes bore witness to a truly architectural order" (OC, I, 177). Of course, this sense of order is imposed by the onlooker. Bataille remembers that "during the early days of childhood, for our generation, the terrifying forms of architecture were . . . those large factory smokestacks" (OC, I, 206). Technology, with its suffocating sense of sacrificial utilitarian production, promises architectural testimony to the human dominance of the landscape. Bataille soon understands, however, that the various styles of architecture were merely attempts to limit human excess and to provide models for what Bataille calls "metaphysical scaffolding" (OC, I, 220). The very discipline of architecture, and the allied studies of physics and engineering, provide metaphors for the structures and superstructures of social existence. The hierarchies and sovereignties among human beings established throughout history and within various civilizations find their justifications in such sciences. Even what Bataille calls "the myth of Freud" (OC, VIII, 28), that is, the psychoanalytical hypothesis of the structuring of the ego, is an internalization of the laws of physics and architecture. In the introduction to the translation of his study of Bataille, appropriately entitled *Against Architecture*,[36] Denis Hollier points out that Bataille's articles in *Documents* in 1929 were also prefigurations of the attitudes against structuralism in the writings of Foucault and Derrida, which are discussed in chapter 4. Hollier also notes, in another article, that architecture for Bataille is anthropomorphic as a model for the imprisoning of the human condition.[37] Architecture is obsessed with forms, and this formal obsession points to the prison as the basic model. This imprisoning of the human mind is the threat of architecture with its structures towering above humanity as reminders of the limitations of human achievement.

Bataille's antiarchitectural stance is balanced by his insights into the unity of human and animal life. Throughout his writings, he develops the view that "animals and humans form a single being" (OC, I, 269). Consequently, they share a common link with life and cannot be formally separated. Although in appearances animals and humans inhabit different communities, Bataille notes that "humanity however does not have a simple architecture as do animals, and it is not even possible to say where humanity begins" (OC, I, 237). Architecture and physics are thus too limited in their scope and do not provide viable insights into the interconnectedness of the human condition.

Instead, Bataille looks toward the sciences that explore myths to see how the vital principles of humanity have been vitiated by giving artificial structure to the social conditions of humanity. During his early career as a librarian, he was interested in the science of numismatics, coin collecting, because coins provided access to ancient myths of the headless god Acéphale, that is, "the chthonian nature of mythic reality which we are examining" (OC, II, 278). On these coins, he found reproductions of humanity that were not structured by laws of geometry and physics. Curiously, the Kinsey Report also intrigued him for similar reasons, that is, that science proves that "humanity is primarily animal" (OC, X, 149). The dreams of architecture, with its imposing facades of human habitation and the laws of physics and engineering governing human construction, only mask humanity within an impossible setting. Bataille's relationship to science is thus an ambivalent one that Allan Stoekl expresses well, delineating how Bataille views science in a post-Hegelian framework by juxtaposing knowing and unknowing: "There is a stable doctrine of un-knowing; non-knowing is absorbed by knowing, just as knowing is absorbed by non-knowing."[38] This intriguing relationship between knowing and unknowing makes Bataille an appealing influence to intellectuals in the twentieth century. Let us now examine the nature of that influence.

## *Chapter Four*

# (Mis)Appropriations of Bataille

Since his death, the writings of Georges Bataille have become crucial to many avant-garde movements. Prior to 1962, his writings did not receive wide acclaim. He was known within a coterie of his followers and within Parisian intellectual circles. Few of his works were translated outside of France, except for his insights into Manet and the Lascaux cave drawings. During his lifetime, he achieved notoriety for the vicious exchange within surrealism with André Breton. He did receive published recognition from both Jean-Paul Sartre and Maurice Blanchot, but these were not fully appreciated until after Bataille's death.

The predominant influence on the appreciation of Bataille's writings was the Tel Quel Group. The Paris-based journal *Tel Quel* was founded in 1960. One of its founders, Philippe Sollers, became a major intellectual force in avant-garde writing through his direction of the journal and its interests.[1] Michel Foucault, Roland Barthes, Julia Kristeva, and others collaborated in 1968 on *Théorie d'Ensemble*, a manifesto of the crucial dogmas of the journal and its contributors. Foucault, Barthes, Sollers, and Denis Hollier then made major contributions to the importance of Bataille's writings and thought in their focus upon a modern conception of writing. Although not formally allied with the Tel Quel Group, Susan Sontag, a close friend of Roland Barthes, later published incisive essays on Bataille for an American audience.

Jacques Derrida, once a member of the Tel Quel Group, forged a specific identity for what he called "deconstruction" and used this attitude toward texts to revisit the insights of Bataille.[2] Likewise, Derrida's respondent in the Frankfurt School, Jürgen Habermas, who continues to advocate a consensus-based view of communication, presented Bataille in light of his literary theories.

During the 1970s and1980s, as a sequel to the May 1968 student and worker riots in Paris, there emerged a sociologically oriented group of writers for whom Bataille speaks loudly. Jean Baudrillard and Pierre Bourdieu have independently developed major thrusts in the evaluation of what has become known as a postmodern culture largely because of the philosophical influence of Jean-François Lyotard. Bataille's writings have figured in a crucial prefiguration of many of the sociological attitudes seen therein. Michael Richardson has also presented Bataille primarily as a sociologist and therefore as a commentator on the cultural evolution of France and the world.

In addition, Bataille has become a major reference for other evolving intellectual positions. He has become a source for those opposing sexist, homophobic, and aesthetic positions. Bataille's work is now widely available in translation in most major languages. Because of his delayed entrance into French avant-garde and intellectual circles during the 1960s and 1970s, his voice is still heard in those circles, and his positions on eroticism, the economy, and repressed sociological behavior continue to inspire. Usually, appreciation of Bataille comes when his work supports the liberal cause of one group or another, usually at the expense of the wide range of Bataille's thought. That wide range is what still allows his work to be appealing to many divergent interests. Let us look at what have been thus far the major recoveries of Bataille's writings and thought.

## André Breton and the Surrealist Program

For many years, Bataille's work was thought to be antisurrealist. After the *Second Manifesto of Surrealism* (1929), in which Breton mocks Bataille's "phobia for the 'idea' " and lack of commitment to surrealism,[3] Bataille continues the mudslinging in *Un Cadavre*, in which the surrealists alienated by Breton strike back together with personal diatribes against him. Bataille justifies his position with the claim that Breton's idealism constructed a "metaphysical scaffolding [which] was of no more interest than the different styles of architecture" (OC, I, 220). For 10 years there seemed to be no reconciliation in their enmity. Bataille felt personally rejected in favor of surrealism by Michel Leiris (OC, VII, 171), who introduced Bataille to Breton in 1924. To this day, some definitions in biographical dictionaries continue to cast Bataille as "antisurrealist."[4]

However, Bataille's actual relationship to both Breton and surrealism is much more complex. Recently, Michael Richardson has promoted the case, through the careful exposition of Bataille's contribution to surrealist causes and expositions, especially the 1947 surrealist exhibition at the Galeries Maeght in Paris and then in Prague.[5] This exhibition involved Bataille's contribution of the essay "The Absence of Myth," and, more importantly, his continued collaboration with Breton. In 1935, Breton and Bataille worked together in *Contre-Attaque* to oppose fascism, which they saw as their common enemy. Breton approved of Bataille's title *Minotaure* for a surrealist journal, and he approvingly heard Bataille lecture after the war. There was undoubtedly a love-hate relationship between the two men. They were similar in style and ambition, if not in attitude toward idealism and materialism. Although Bataille was opposed to Breton's direction of surrealism, he remained surrealist in spirit. Bataille maintained an ongoing relationship with Antonin Artaud, whose ideas were likewise irreconcilable with Breton's plan for surrealism. Nevertheless, Breton continued to keep Bataille out of the inner circle of surrealist doctrine. The negative energy between the two contributed and still contributes to Bataille's status as a marginalized intellectual hero.

## Blanchot and Sartre during the War

In contrast to the enmity with Breton, Blanchot's friendship with Bataille proved to be very fruitful in terms of helping the critical reception of Bataille's writings. Although Bataille's critical reception in France may have been impeded by the confusion of ideological, political, and intellectual direction in Paris at the onset of World War II, certainly Blanchot, characterized by Libertson as "Bataille's most important interlocutor" (123), was generous to his newfound friend. He promoted Bataille's work and still continues to place Bataille's writings on the cutting edge of literary experimentation with insights into the impossible, plural voices, and a Nietzschean affirmation of the radical questioning of the limits of human experience (Blanchot, 1969, 302–10). Blanchot continued to support Bataille's work after the war, especially during the difficult days of keeping the journal *Critique* from being neglected for its support of avant-garde philosophical and literary ventures. Blanchot also gave crucial critical reception to some of Bataille's "obscene" works, such as *Madame Edwarda* (Blanchot, 1983, 80 ff.), although this support came only after Bataille's death. During the war, Blanchot, as well as Jean-Paul Sartre, an important voice critiquing Bataille, published often and with prestigious presses. Blanchot came to be known for his perceptive literary criticism and theory. While he resided in the Unoccupied Zone in southern France, he was writing and then publishing his work in Paris. Blanchot's *Faux pas*[6] included a chapter on Bataille's *L'Expérience intérieure* and identified nonknowledge and anguish as being key areas to be developed in the neo-Nietzschean period of philosophy.

Jean-Paul Sartre also found Bataille's *L'Expérience intérieure* worthy of a chapter, though for reasons different than those of Blanchot. In the first volume of Sartre's *Situations*, Bataille becomes Sartre's "straw man" for his own theory of committed literature. Bataille is the "new mystic" who is "anti-intellectual" and yet who has retained from his devout Christian past a profound respect for historicity (Sartre, *Situations,* 148). Certainly, Bataille would not be seen as anti-intellectual by today's standards. Sartre is referring to the abstract understanding of mysticism from which Bataille is trying to distinguish himself. Sartre thought himself superior to Bataille, was not enthusiastic about Bataille's arguments about laughter, and found Bataille's arguments too serious in tone. For Sartre, Bataille is able to make his reader experience the laughter that enables the relief from the anguish and shame of base materialism and the abyss of nothingness.

Bataille answered Sartre by delineating his position as an intellectual distinct from Sartre's politically involved model. Bataille refused to be the complete man that Sartre's totalistic enterprise claims as a model, as he states that "I cannot be a holistic man, I subordinate myself to a specific goal: to become everything [*le tout*]" (OC, VI, 202). This ideal of *le tout* is an intellectual ideal that is an alternative to Sartre's political criterion. Jean-Michel Besnier aptly distinguishes Bataille's "desire to be incorporated in the body of history more strongly than that of carrying out a political manifesto" ("Intellectual," 17) as both Sartre and Breton prefer to see themselves doing. In 1957, in an interview with Marguerite Duras, Bataille notes about himself that "I lack the vocation of those who feel responsible for the world" (21). Instead, the journal *Critique*, with its focus on international literary and philosophical ventures, was Bataille's response to Sartre's *Les Temps modernes*. Sartre provided Bataille with the counterpoint for his own identity. Despite the lack of positive reinforcement from Sartre, Bataille began to define himself from the criticism he received from Sartre. Bataille would even go so far as to speculate that "[Whereas] Sartre speaks of *action*, is this sufficient? Is it not even the worst [course]?" (OC, XI, 252). Other reactions to Sartre's program would begin to create even more positive appreciation of Bataille's writings.

## Spinoffs from *Tel Quel*

The founding of the journal *Tel Quel* in 1960 brought together a group of people for whom, individually and collectively, the writings of Bataille were signal achievements. In this group, I will discuss Michel Foucault,

Roland Barthes, Susan Sontag, and Philippe Sollers. Although Susan Sontag was not a member of the Tel Quel Group, she was influenced by her friendship with Barthes and his appreciation of Bataille. Jacques Derrida also contributed to *Tel Quel* from 1965 to 1967. However, I will discuss his appreciation of Bataille in a separate section on deconstruction.

Michel Foucault's recuperation of Bataille becomes a basis for the Foucauldian arguments for the relationships of knowledge and social power. In Foucault's 1963 article in *Critique,* he praises Bataille's experimentation with the impossible, with nudity, eroticism, and the limits imposed by taboo.[7] From Bataille's writings, Foucault learns that "contesting means going right to the empty heart where being confronts its limits and where limitation defines being" (Foucault, 756). The "empty heart" is what Foucault himself struggles with in all of his writings, that is, the core of human nature, which has been disguised and denied by the social codification of restrictions. Bataille's repudiation of the social strictures of sovereignty in the Middle Ages is developed in Foucault's *Folie et déraison* (1961). Bataille's thought is interspersed throughout Foucault's work and becomes a basic theoretical reference for Foucault's own writings on negativity in examining social attitudes toward madness, criminal imprisonment, and sexuality. Bataille's questioning attitude toward the imposition of arbitrary limitations upon human thought inspires Foucault to wonder about the possibility of philosophy itself being a mad discipline in that the parameters for social discourse are probably found in what Bataille spoke of as the opposition between "the order of things" and "the intimate order" (OC, VII, 343 ff.) of the human heart. However, as Michael Richardson delineates, Foucault is not completely in line with Bataille in that, in contrast to Foucault's vision, "The denial of individualism was not an issue for Bataille: what was important was to contest its totalizing impulse" (Richardson, *Bataille,* 46). Bataille's adaptation of Nietzschean sovereignty is also ignored in favor of a focus on Foucault's agenda. Nevertheless, Bataille's writings do become a focus of attention for Foucault as he opens the way for his colleagues in the Tel Quel Group to reveal the many sides of Bataille's writings.

Roland Barthes focuses on the literary work of Bataille to provide an example for Barthesian literary semiology. Barthes shifts the attention away from Bataille's theoretical work toward his creative opus. Specifically, Barthes wrote two essays expanding upon Bataille's "L'Histoire de l'oeil" (1928) and "le Gros Orteil" (1929). Both essays are in the mold of Barthes's formalist demythologizing of French ideology as in his *Mytho-*

*logies* (1957). Essentially, he takes the repetition of basic images such as the eye and the big toe as representative of a view of language that uses metonymy to question metaphor as the access to a rarefied world of intellectual symbols. On the one hand, he implements a formalist description of the eye in "L'Histoire de l'oeil" to explain Bataille's literary style as one in which the erotic manifests itself in a grounding of the text in a story structuring surfaces without hierarchies,[8] this being another version of Barthes's own view of a narrative unfolding like an onion with no kernel. However, Barthes also effectively ignores Bataille's symbolic system of mystical and ritualistic atheology.[9] Such a surface reading of Bataille also inspires Susan Sontag's reading of the aesthetic value of Bataille's creative writings in 1967.[10] On the other hand, when Barthes analyzed "Le Gros Orteil," which he did for a *Tel Quel* symposium on Bataille at Cerisy-la-Salle in 1972, he acknowledged Bataille's insights into the "amorous rhythm" of knowledge and value,[11] thus implying that there are ethical assertions within Bataille's writings. The amorous rhythm became a major component of Barthes's later work as he literally implemented Bataille's insights into fragmentation as the enemy of coherent thought with the Barthesian focus on the essay.[12] When "Le Gros Orteil" was published under Bataille's name in *Documents*, it created a scandal at the Bibliothèque nationale[13] that may have resulted in Bataille's demotion to the medals section. Hence, Barthes is correct to note that the issue of social values is indeed one of the stakes in Bataille's creative writing. As Bataille himself asserts, "The big toe is the most *human* part of the human body" because it "has its foot in the mud" but "its head is practically in the light" (OC, I, 200). There are mystical, that is, intellectual, stakes to Bataille's base materialism that Barthes suggested and Philippe Sollers enjoyed developing.

Sollers makes Bataille into an icon of the theory and practice of writing as promoted by the journal *Tel Quel* during the late 1960s and early 1970s. It was probably Sollers who encouraged Barthes to analyze Bataille's writings. During the late 1960s Sollers published several crucial essays promoting the importance of Bataille's theories on expense, the sacred, and base materialism as parameters for a materialistic type of writing.[14] The culmination of this promotion, the 1972 symposium at Cerisy-la-Salle, followed by the Sollers-edited volume *Bataille* in 1973, gave voices to Jean-Louis Baudry, Denis Hollier, and Jean-Louis Houdebine, all of whom promote two types of communication fostered by Bataille, principally though language and through expenditure. Sollers prefers to focus upon Bataille's "practices" of communication. These practices—that is, Bataille's vision of the sacred, sex, the general economy, and writing—are developed in various essays by Sollers. Bataille comes forth in Sollers as a much more ideologically aligned writer than he appears when reading him. For example, Sollers promotes Bataille as exemplifying the growth of expenditure, with such an example as the antihero of *Le Bleu du ciel* offering "a kind of permanent invitation to decomposition" (Sollers, *Guerre,* 456) while "the negative laughs" (Sollers, *Bataille,* 17) at the various utilitarian attempts to recuperate human communication. The result is that Sollers offers his systematic ideological model of Bataille that is much more totalistic than what Bataille himself ever tries to accomplish.

More interesting is the encouragement that *Tel Quel* has given to various writers who bring out the importance of Bataille's less systematic tendencies. For example, Denis Hollier has dedicated his lifework to the collected works of Bataille and to pointing out that Bataille's materialistic dualism rests upon the dualism between morality and beyond good and evil.[15] His beginnings with *Tel Quel* continue to bear fruit in his many essays on Bataille. Another enlightened reader of Bataille found in *Tel Quel* is Bernard Sichère, who provides especially insightful perspectives on Bataille's eroticism and points out that "Bataille's writing makes us aware of a very dear anguish of 'becoming a woman' which is undoubtedly the most hidden core of the masculine unconscious."[16] We shall return to this theme of gender association and ethics in Bataille in chapter 5. However, another early associate of the Tel Quel Group should be mentioned for his contributions to the Bataille legacy: Jacques Derrida. Since Derrida took Bataille's writings into another dimension, let us consider Bataille as a component of what is now called deconstruction.

## Deconstructing Bataille

Jacques Derrida finds some natural alliance in Bataille's theories. Derrida, whose perspective called deconstruction has focused on the blind spots in a writer's work, is attracted to Bataille, who notes that "understanding is a blind task which recalls the structure of the eye" (OC, V, 129). Rather than the metonymical eye that becomes the formalistic model for Barthes, the blinded eye attracts Derrida in his perspective. Derrida is also intrigued by the word communication, which for him "opens a semantic field which precisely is not limited to semantics, semiotics, and even less to linguistics."[17] Here again, Bataille offers Derrida a writer who is concerned with communication in its alinguistic character and is an anti-Hegelian Hegelian. In an essay (Derrida, 24–44) reprinted in *L'Écriture et la différence* (1967), Derrida repudiates Sartre's claim that Bataille is a "new mystic" and looks to Bataille for a Hegelianism that is not teleologically driven by synthesis. Derrida proposes to read Bataille against Bataille by arguing that Bataille is not as Hegelian as he thinks he is. In effect, Derrida claims that Bataille's example as a writer and philosopher rests upon Bataille's view that "only laughter can exceed the dialectic and the dialectician" (Sollers, *Bataille,* 28). Jürgen Habermas, who opposes deconstruction from the Frankfurt School position, takes exception to this reading of Bataille.

Habermas is an advocate of context as the primary criterion of what he calls Critical Theory. Habermas adapts Bataille's theory of human sovereignty to a Marxian agenda in which sovereignty means "not to let oneself be reduced, as in labor, to the condition of an object, but to free subjectivity from bondage."[18] Critical Theory is the attempt to provide a postmodern reply to Derrida's deconstruction. For Habermas, context is crucial and entails a version of what he calls consensus, that is, responsiveness to the community of listeners he is addressing. He challenges Derrida's assertion that "there is no context" and, within such a challenge, calls up Bataille as a theoretician of fascist heterogeneity. Bataille did not do enough to assert himself in his own political context of the rising threat of fascism during the 1930s in France. Habermas views Bataille's theories as "having sensed this dilemma but did not resolve it."[19] For Habermas, Bataille set up the problem of the utilitarian agenda for modernity but did not go far enough, that is, "Bataille undercut his own efforts to carry out the radical critique of reason with the tools of theory" (Habermas, *Discourse,* 237). Habermas sees Bataille as having flirted too much with fascism and its ties between reason and political power and thus was caught up in the "dialectic of the enlightenment," the modern problem isolated by the first generation of the Frankfurt School, specifically Theodor Adorno and Max Horkheimer, who attended sessions of the *Collège de Sociologie*. Bataille's resurrection by sociologists such as Horkheimer, however, goes much further than Habermas projects. Jean Baudrillard especially bears witness to elaborate developments of Bataille's sociological insights.

## Sociological Variations

Once Bataille identified himself with the *Collège de Sociologie,* he opened the door for professional sociologists to examine closely his theories and observations.[20] Pierre Bourdieu (*Esquisse d'une théorie de la pratique*, 1972) acknowledges the importance of Bataille's sociological theories of sacrifice, eroticism, the general economy, and community. Michael Richardson (*Georges Bataille*, 1994) continues to believe that Bataille's principal identity is in the area of sociology. Jean Baudrillard has taken exception to the rising popularity of Bataille's sociology. During the 1970s, Baudrillard moved Bataille's theories into debates about the issues of what has come to be called postmodernism, the philosophical position introduced by Jean-François Lyotard (*La Condition postmoderne*, 1979) that pointed toward outmoded narratives explaining the human condition and the ways in which knowledge is acquired and demanded new paradigms for learning. In a 1976 review of the publication of volume 7 of Bataille's collected works in French, Baudrillard claims that Bataille's thought is unified by its economic insights into the human condition. He also says that Bataille misread Mauss's theory of gifts to mean that there can be a unilateral gift; Bataille is too focused on the individual's inner economic drives rather than on the interaction of the individual in a social economic context. Hence, Baudrillard believes that Bataille is mistaken because "the root of sacrifice and the general economy is never pure and simple expenditure. . . ."[21] Economic forces are not merely internal, according to Baudrillard, who has busily set up the capitalistic consequences of Lyotard's postmodern vision. Of course, Bataille's theories are still being displaced into an electronic global village about which he had no clue during his lifetime. Yet Baudrillard placed Bataille's texts in the reading environment of postmodern, postcolonial, and capitalistic conditions.

Baudrillard also considers Bataille's views on death worthy of sociological debate. Bataille's relationship of eroticism and death has been especially attractive to psychoanalytical interpretations of the postmodern sociological situation. Baudrillard points out that Bataille stresses the metaphysical continuity between eroticism and death and as a result death becomes a principle of "anti-economy,"[22] as does eroticism whereby "we renounce death and accumulate rather than lose ourselves" (Baudrillard, *Échange,* 237). To go beyond psychoanalysis, as Bataille sometimes tries to do with his mystical visions for the order of things, may be too ambitious a metaphysical project for a postmodern sociology that can learn much from Bataille in the here-and-now reality.

Baudrillard is much inspired by Bataille's economic and erotic theories of society. While sometimes Bataille's base materialism focuses too much on the reification of gifts, Baudrillard develops the insight that the very acts of giving and receiving within a general economy become types of social communication.[23] Also from Bataille's view of eroticism as transgression of taboos that must remain despite their being superseded, Baudrillard notes that nudity has become a type of clothing by assuming the cultural value of a ludic community that sees itself as free from the repressive taboos of reproductive sex. This nudity is also behind the masks that we wear as social beings, the masks that are so important in Bataille's creative and theoretical writings. Baudrillard concludes that "it is the mask which makes sacrifice possible, which allows us to make war, the mask which enables us to engage in politics."[24] The sociopolitical arena, which many have thought Bataille abandoned for his intellectual endeavors, is a rich one in terms of Baudrillard's investigations of the postmodern setting of Bataille's writings.

Others have also expanded the political end of Bataille's sociopolitical applications in the last quarter of the twentieth century. Two major applications are investigations into the nature of community and feminist theoretical and creative practices. Jean-Luc Nancy has been one of the principal theoreticians of rethinking community, arriving as a consequence of the Holocaust and various types of xenophobia and racism that have manifested themselves despite the creation of political agencies dedicated to the identification and neutralization of hate groups. Nancy places Bataille's reflections on the nature of community at the center of discussion because of Bataille's theories of the space of community outside of itself, that is, the capability of realizing a space outside the confines of how it sees itself.[25] This concept is crucial for the social tolerance of the Other and for the welcoming of the Other into community so that plural, working communities will become a reality. Bataille's vision of personal ecstasy and community placed him away from where Nancy would like contemporary political thinkers to be,[26] that is, within the ideal of a tolerant, open community. Nevertheless, as with Baudrillard's presentation of Bataille, Nancy's Bataille is taking us even beyond where Bataille himself thought we should be.

The feminist rearrangement of Bataille is curious in light of Bataille's sometimes sexist positions. Given Dominique de Roux's insight that "Tantrism is merely the employment of woman as an instrument,"[27] Bataille's attraction to tantric cults and the virile motifs of his writing do not make an especially attractive feminist voice. Benoîte Groult has observed, for example, that, despite the claim that Bataille is presenting a more frank view of human eroticism, the word "clitoris" is absent from his presentations of women's sexuality.[28] Such shortcomings, as well as

# *Chapter Five*
# Overlooked Affirmations

My many endnotes containing references to the scholarship on Bataille attest to the great academic interest that Bataille's writings have elicited throughout the world. Nevertheless, his work contains many affirmations that have yet to be developed by those intrigued by what he has to say. I organize this discussion around five major themes in Bataille that hold promise as worthy of being developed. First, Bataille's concerns about utility are especially poignant for capitalist endeavors. Although his arguments are addressed to a culture of bourgeois values, his alternatives are viable for capitalists likewise overly concerned with utility. Second, the transgression of utility leads me to Bataille's arguments for what I call "a community of dis-order" wherein Bataille argues for gender differentiation as principles of subversion to the existing models of relationships. Third, within such a community, Bataille presents asymmetrical giving as a positive way to reinforce self-selected community. Fourth, Bataille argues for a view of myth as a way for humankind to think analogically. Within his view of community, such myths are valuable means of personal and social expression. Last, Bataille offers the possibility for an ethics of reading that is a means of pursuing unity and communion in communication. All five of these affirmations read Bataille against and with Bataille's conscious self.

## Alternatives to Capitalism

Bataille often poses laughter in opposition to the homogeneity of the French bourgeois comfort with respectability. One of the problems with surrealism was its dependence upon the bourgeois to buy the paintings that expressed its revolutionary stance. Bataille did not put a price on great poetry and its ties with the sacred and laughed in *Un Cadavre* at Breton's pseudosanctity for the surrealist movement. Laughter thus enabled Bataille to escape from Western culture's subservience to utility. In *Madame Edwarda*, his narrator tells us that "laughter is no longer respectful, but it's the sign of horror; laughter is the attitude of compromise which a human adopts in the presence of a perspective which is repulsive when this perspective does not appear to be serious" (OC, III, 9–10). Bourgeois stances often leave Bataille laughing because of their lack of seriousness about community.

Capitalism deserves the same kind of reaction from the "authentic writer," an identity Bataille gives himself as teaching "the refusal of usefulness" (OC, XI, 13). Elsewhere, he speaks of his mission as the "modern writer {who} can only be linked with productive society by requiring it to have a surplus wherein the utility principle can no longer reign . . ." (OC, XII, 28). Like the bourgeoisie with its assumed aristocratic postures, capitalists pose the same kind of threat to humanity, that of homogeneity in the utilitarian attitude toward capital. Bataille traces the origins of sovereignty in the feudal hierarchical society passed on during the origins of capitalism. Curiously, Bernard-Henri Lévy observes the manifest ties between feudalism and capitalism in the social structure of modern Pakistan, which was formed by British imperialist projections of a modern Islamic state and remains as a testimony of human sovereignty.[1] In 1948, Bataille could see that "we are enclosed in a capitalist world" (Richardson, *Absence,* 79), but he did not think it was his responsibility to suppress this capitalist reality. Capitalist industrialist reality, after all, remained from his childhood as providing him with images of base materialism in the factory smokestacks: "veritable pipes of communication between the sky which was so sinisterly dirty and the muddy earth" (OC, I, 206). Here is where the laughable enters. Bataille sees that "the laughable is usually the object of a sentiment of superiority on the part of the one who laughs" (OC, XI, 542). The sovereignty of the one who laughs enables the subject of capitalism to transcend the interest of capital, the greed of savings, of surplus, and to look instead toward a community envisioned in Bataille's mystical moments. The values of expenditure toward others, a general economic attitude toward generosity, could modify the self-implosive destructive utility of capitalism that survives as testimony to the socialized principles of sovereignty that was part of the late feudal system. Bataille offers alternate models for a community to go beyond the sovereignty of capital.

## A Community of Dis-Order

In his promotion of the heterology and discontinuity of life, Bataille expressed his ambition to totalize, that is, to impose a homogeneous and idealistic vision, despite his overt rejection of totalizing as a way of controlling how people think and live in a community. His views of women and the relationships between women qua women and men are especially pertinent to this sense of community. I have already mentioned how his overuse of the words **impuissance** and **virilité** indicate a male-centered universe, the perspective of the "prickly eye" [**l'oeil pinéal**] in which women are marginalized. Regarding the woman's role in heterosexual relationships, the narrator in "La Venus de Lespugue" tells us that "in general a man does not want to possess a woman while becoming the object of her desire" (OC, IX, 350). It is not surprising to recognize the popularity of Bataille's writings in male homosexual communities and also the repulsiveness feminists feel toward this lack of sensitivity to women's perspectives on male sexuality and women's views on sexuality in general.

What appears to be a single-minded sexist perspective, however, must be qualified by Bataille's portrayal of women's views of sexuality in his creative writings. Sometimes his narrators are female prostitutes (e.g., "La Houpette," OC, IV, 333–34; also his poems, IV, 29 and 30) expressing their views about sexuality; sometimes his male narrators present the debauchery of women (e.g., *Le Mort* and *Ma Mère*). Granted, these presentations are about women who are marginalized, as prostitutes or as a deranged mother. Nevertheless, Bataille is a male writer who thus acknowledges the limitations and anxiety of "responses to the most virile concerns" (OC, I, 523). In his *Divinus Deus*, Bataille's narrator speaks of Madeleine as a woman content in her gendered lifestyle: "She often told me that she was happy to be a woman because a woman, especially a beautiful and a rich one, could live in the most provocative way on the condition that she feared no shame and that, on the contrary, she could find her sensual pleasure in her shame" (OC, IV, 291). Of course, some could say that only in being marginalized as a woman could Madeleine be happy. But indeed Bataille speaks similarly about men qua men, that is, that they have to transcend the gender roles that society, with its sovereign rules, has assigned. In these transgressions, which Bataille calls eroticism, individuals attain mystical communication with each other. Hence, creative disorder in gender roles is what leads to gifts within relationships between men and women. Let us look at Bataille's view of giving. He adapts Marcel Mauss's anthropological views of gifts as theories of economic exchange by going one step further to view gifts as a way to change the known order and to create an entry into a new type of community. This adaptation is worthy of discussion.

## Asymmetrical Giving

Bataille's theory of expenditure in a general economy as an alternative to the utility of savings in surplus economies places the gift in a special position within communities. While Marcel Mauss views potlatch within "mechanisms of obligation, and even of obligation through things, that are called into play" (Mauss, 23), Bataille expands upon this playfulness to call into question the retributive sense of justice that belies most theologically based communities. His sense of the sacred focuses on communication that does not expect recompense: "Even today the ideal should be that, once potlatch is given, that it be impossible to return it" (OC, VII, 203).

This impossibility of returning the gift assumes an asymmetrical generosity upon which Bataille's sense of community is founded. In Bataille's studies of the Incas and Mayas, he finds that "generosity, in the former Mexico, was one of the attributes of the sovereign, of the 'human chief' " (OC, VII, 199). Hence, an asymmetrical generosity gives natural sovereignty to humanity. Similar to the asymmetrical ethical obligation to the Other developed by Emmanuel Lévinas (*Totalité et Infini*, 1961),[2] Bataille's attitude toward giving finds very specific political causes such as his support of the Marshall Plan after World War II. Although he recognized that the plan had capitalist greed at stake (OC, XI, 371), he advocated its implementation for its generous expenditure and the sense of communication as communion that it could instill in world community. Bataille's mystical vision of communication is worth recalling: "Communicating means trying to achieve unity and being many within one, which has finally come to mean *communion*" (OC, VI, 279). Although the Marshall Plan was an imperialistic move by capitalist states, Bataille acknowledges that ". . . we need sovereign values because it is *useful* to have useless ideas" (Bataille, *L'Agonie,* 17). Community, so crucial to the respect for the sacred and the mystical sense of unity that the common practice of rituals achieves, appears to be more important to Bataille than the total rejection of usefulness. Certainly, there is utility in eroticism that, through a communal sense of generosity, "would no longer be *in the margins of history*" (OC, VIII, 163). Such a communal view of generosity exists for Bataille not only in action but also in the stories that such a community tells about itself, that is, its myths. Hence, Bataille's view of myth is also a crucial component of the survival of a community based on generosity.

## Myth and Analogical Thinking

Of course, the Acéphale is the myth usually associated with Bataille's atheological community. This myth gives coherence to both the individual and the community to which one belongs. On the one hand, the Acéphale is worthy of being at the core of Bataille's mythology due to the lack of external sovereignty in the sacredness associated with the Acéphale: "Beyond what I am, I encounter a being which makes me laugh because it is headless and which fills me with anguish because it is filled with innocence and crime" (OC, I, 445). The anguish recalls the adolescent boy who is the narrator of *Ma Mère* and who speaks about learning "ignominy" from his mother when she conveys a change in attitude since his innocent youth about his masturbation (Bataille, *Mère,* 32). The narrator claims that at that moment an abyss opened between himself and his mother. The abyss provides another mythological element in how an individual is distinguished within a community. The abyss is an analogy about the external separation of the child from family and the anguished individuation leading toward death.

On the other hand, the myths of a community also give the individual the masks of laughter. Bataille derives some consolation (OC, V, 60) from the motto of Descartes, also later cherished by Roland Barthes: *larvatus prodeo,* "I advance pointing to my mask." The mask allows the individual to displace the individuation of personal death and the anguish of the proximity of the abyss. Laughter, not only as a personal but also as a communal experience with friends and associates, provides analogical distance from anxiety and makes communication easier according to Bataille. While "laughter has the virtue of provoking laughter" (OC, VII, 274), a social setting for communication ensues. Bataille thus believes that "our laughs constantly make communications in our life easy" (OC, VII, 272).

Mythology provides the stories for communities to narrate about themselves and by which communities can laugh at themselves together. Bataille believes in the human community and the presence of others to console the individual in the face of death. In the 1957 trial to determine whether Pauvert should be allowed to publish the Marquis de Sade's writings, Bataille answered the posturing of the prosecutor, Maurice Garçon, about the serious threat of Sade's writings to the morals of society: "I must say that I have great confidence in human nature" (OC, XII, 456). This confidence has to do with the interpretations of Sade's fiction into myths about the limitations that taboos gleaned from righteous guidelines about morality have placed on human thinking.

Bataille also provides creative writing that transgresses those taboos. In effect, his stories are examples of myths about human fantasies rather than transcendent gods or divine intervention in human affairs. His interest in nonknowledge is a similar extension into analogical thinking, that is, what would human communities be like if certain conditions existed. Hence, mythology inhabits what we, as humans, do not know about ourselves in areas such as fear, humiliation, pain, violence—those regions of experience inhabited by tears and laughter that are outside cognitive reality and yet within the experience of a mystical community willing to probe what lies beyond generosity. This kind of community promises ethical perspectives that are worth examining.

## Toward an Ethics of Reading

Bataille rejects his work as philosophy. He does, however, promote an attitude that can be called the communal revolt or rebellion against boundaries. One person acts in concert with others who together respect the sacredness of going beyond restrictions and in that transgression find a common mystical experience. At one point, Bataille speaks about the pale as representing for him the attitude of such an individual: "I cannot conceive of my life any more except as nailed to the *extreme of what is possible*" (OC, V, 51). One should be impaled to the attitude of pushing the limits of the possible. This attitude has components that place the individual in relationship to the others of a community and provide guidelines for identifying obstacles that limit the achievement of such a community.

First, Bataille realizes that cognitive learning does not give one access to a mystical community. The ethics of this community is read as an apparent object of intelligence but "becomes the object of ecstasy—the object of tears and the object of laughter" (OC, I, 510). For Bataille, to laugh is to read ethically and mystically because the impulse to laugh is a result of insight into the human condition and the boundaries of propriety. In Bataille's "Julie," Suzanne sees Henri's father at the bedside of his son, who has just committed suicide, and she laughs aloud. She then explains that it was a nervous reaction (OC, IV, 93). Her laughter gives her a glimpse into the impropriety of a father surviving his son and being at his son's deathbed. Her need to excuse her laugh as biologically driven is the community's influence on her to halt the tendency of her sovereignty toward solipsism. She expresses compassion for the father while pointing to the transgression of a social code made by her body.

Laughter is valuable as a personal manifestation of the need to go beyond the limitations of a moment, effectively to create one's own ethical bonds. Bataille argues that "laughter is the foundation of everything provided that it is a question of laughing about oneself . . ." (Chapsal, 236). Laughter is to be understood as the reaction of the self not being comfortable with its context. In the silence after laughter, the self is revealed (OC, X, 270). For Bataille, the individual then finds a better role among others in a self-defined community: "If we are more involved in participation which is not clearly conscious to the shared activity, this is the best part of ourselves" (OC, XII, 29). Recognition by others would make participation a desired symmetrical activity. Therefore, it is better that the individual act communally without interest but merely because personal sovereignty must be balanced with "the necessity to accept the existence of others and to respect it entirely" (Duras, 21). This openness toward others goes beyond tolerance by making otherness a mandate for change in the self. This mandate became an ethical principle for Bataille's agenda for the *Acéphale,* the name he gave to the secret society he formed in 1937: "Secretly or not, it is necessary to become totally as others are or to cease to exist" (OC, I, 443). This is quite a challenge as we read not only texts but the cultures in which we find ourselves. Bataille would have us find our individual sovereignty through this ability to interact such that we could become Other without the acknowledgment that this is a generous act for the good of the community. This is part of the struggle of reading Bataille's writings because he is caught up in the tension between the need for the self to assert its independence from cultural limitations and the need to participate in the communion of community. Marguerite Duras prophetically states the challenge of Bataille as one of those writers people put off reading: "People continue to live with the illusion that they will one day be able to speak about Bataille . . . they will die without having dared."[3] In response to Duras's bold situation of the potential readers of Bataille's often outrageous writings, we should consider the alternatives: to dare to read Bataille is to dare to live ethically and to face death in a sovereign way.

# Notes and References

*Preface*

1. Denis Hollier, in *Bataille,* ed. Philippe Sollers (Paris: Union Générale d'Editions, 1973), 103: "une espêce de potlatch verbal." On the same page, he continues: "Il n'est en fait jamais possible quand on parle de Bataille de s'asseoir sur un mot, même sur deux. Il y a un mouvement constant du vocabulaire" ("In fact, when speaking of Bataille, it has never been possible to rely on one word, or even two. There is a continual movement in his vocabulary").

*Chapter One*

1. Georges Bataille, *Oeuvres complètes,* Volume VII, ed. Thadée Klossowski (Paris: Gallimard, 1976), 397: "Je vous ai trouvé catholique à certains moments." Henceforth, in the text I will cite Bataille's writings from his complete works with the initials OC followed by the volume number and page number. See also Allan Stoekl, "Recognition in *Madame Edwarda,*" in *Bataille: Writing the Sacred,* ed. Carolyn Bailey Gill (London: Routledge, 1995), 77–90 for a discussion of the substitution of profane models of Roman Catholicism's rituals of the sacred in Bataille's fiction.

2. For an intriguing discussion of the incest by Pierre Angélique and his mother in *Ma Mère* as the story of Bataille's own "disguised patricide" (p. 192), see Maryline Lukacher, *Maternal Fictions: Stendhal, Sand, Rachilde, and Bataille* (Durham, N.C.: Duke University Press, 1994), 161–97.

3. Michel Surya, *Georges Bataille, la mort à l'oeuvre,* rev. ed. (Paris: Gallimard, 1992), 12.

4. See especially Bataille's role as a shaman as discussed by Michael Richardson in *Georges Bataille* (London: Routledge, 1994), 112–14.

5. Georges Bataille, *Eponine* (Paris: Les Amis des Editions de Minuit, 1949), 7.

6. Surya (56) notes that this is not the same Spain as the one Bataille speaks about later, for example, in his *Le Bleu du ciel* (1935) with its political intrigue in the face of fascism. The Spain that Bataille encounters in 1922 is a sensual place dominated by the sun, bullfights, and a materialism about which he had not yet reflected. This is the Spain that is the background for his *Histoire de l'oeil* (1928).

7. Georges Bataille, "Letter to René Char on the Incompatibilities of the Writer," tr. Christopher Cartsen, *Yale French Studies,* no. 78 (1990): 35.

8. This is the title of chapter 6 in Miguel de Unamuno, *The Tragic Sense of Life in Men and Nations,* tr. Anthony Kerrigan (Princeton: Princeton University Press, 1972), 118–45.

9. Michel Leiris, *Brisées: Broken Branches,* tr. Lydia Davis (San Francisco: North Point Press, 1989), 237.

10. Michael Richardson, Introduction to his translation of Georges Bataille, *The Absence of Myth: Writings on Surrealism* (London: Verso, 1994), 2–27.

11. Bernard-Henri Lévy (*Les Aventures de la liberté* [Paris: Grasset, 1991], 229 ff.) notes the presence of these four Maklès sisters among a group of intellectuals who had an effect upon their time. The roles among these women have yet to be delineated but is ripe for being exposed insofar as their marriages give them links to the richness of the intellectual, political, sociological, economic, and ideological development of the period between the Wars.

12. See the stakes of this story as a humorous anecdote in my article "The Engendered Blow Job: Bakhtin's Comic Dismemberment and the Pornography of Georges Bataille's 'Story of the Eye' (1928)," *Humor* 3, no. 2 (1990): 177–90.

13. For a presentation of Lascaux as the locus of Bataille's interests in the questions of the relationships among writing, discipline, and authority, see Steven Ungar, "Phantom Lascaux: Origin of the Work of Art," *Yale French Studies,* no. 78 (1990): 246–62.

14. The title "Un Cadavre" was used by the Surrealists in 1924 in response to the death of Anatole France. The use of the same title against Breton in 1930 is a deliberate mocking of Breton's "idealistic" posture regarding what surrealism should be.

15. Jean Piel verifies (*La Rencontre et la différence,* [Paris: Fayard, 1982], 156) that Bataille joins his contemporaries in believing in "la définitive impuissance de la démocratie [pour] combattre le fascisme."

16. Georges Bataille, "L'Agonie (Fragments de Journal)," *Gramma: Ecriture et lecture,* no. 1 (Fall 1974): 8. There is also a peculiar scene in which Bataille recalls his masturbating in front of his dead mother's body (OC, IV, 434; and OC, III, "Le Petit"). He describes this act as "the tribute of a man without God who knows toward which abyss tends the sexually excited body" (OC, II, 130).

17. Bataille planned to write a book entitled *Le Fascisme en France* (Surya, 221), but it was never completed. Nonetheless, the question of whether Bataille was a fascist continues to haunt the scholarship on Bataille, e.g., Allan Stoekl, "Truman's Apotheosis: Bataille, 'Planism,' and Headlessness," *Yale French Studies,* no. 78 (1990): 181–205.

18. Maurice Blanchot, who does not often get personal in his writings, speaks about his daily meetings with Bataille in 1940 when Bataille outspokenly expressed his regret about the article on fascism and his horror about Nazism, Pétain's regime, and the ideologies that accompanied them. Blanchot, "Les Intellectuels en question," *Le Débat* 29 (1984): 20, n. 7.

19. See, for example, Jean-François Fourny, *Introduction à la lecture de Georges Bataille* (New York: Peter Lang, 1988), 54: "... Laure est en un sens à l'origine de la plupart des textes écrits par Bataille pendant les années trente ..."

20. For a discussion of this "failure" of *Masses,* see Marina Galletti, "*Masses*: A Failed College?", tr. Lawrence R. Schehr, *Stanford French Review* 12, no. 1 (Spring 1988): 49–74.

21. Georges Bataille, "Attraction and Repulsion I: Tropisms, Sexuality, Laughter, and Tears," lecture given on 22 January 1938, in Denis Hollier, *The College of Sociology, 1937–39,* tr. Betsy Wing (Minneapolis: University of Minnesota Press, 1988), 104.

22. See Michael Richardson's compelling discussion of Bataille's interests as sociological ones in his *Georges Bataille.*

23. Georges Bataille, *Lettres à Roger Caillois: 4 août 1935–4 février 1959,* ed. Jean-Pierre Le Bouler (Paris: Folle Avoine, 1987), 96.

24. Maurice Blanchot, *La Communauté inavouable* (Paris: Minuit, 1983), 30.

25. "Program (Relative to *Acéphale*)," *October,* no. 36 (Spring 1986): 79.

26. A reproduction of this sketch, dated 1935, can be found in *October,* no. 36 (Spring 1986): 131. The sketch presents a naked, headless male form with outstretched arms. A skull (Bataille claims to have placed a skull at the Place de la Concorde in 1936 in memory of Louis XVI) is found where the penis and testicles would otherwise be. The intestines are drawn in the form of a Daedalian labyrinth (Bataille did suggest the title "Minotaure" for the surrealist journal he founded in 1932 to 1933). In one hand is a dagger pointing upward, in the other a flaming heart. Two stars are found on the deity's chest in the place of human nipples. For an explanation of the gnostic symbolism of this figure, see, in this same journal, parts of the essay by Allen S. Weiss, "Impossible Sovereignty: Between *The Will to Power* and *The Will to Chance,*" *October,* no. 36 (Spring 1986): 130–36.

27. Laure, *Ecrits: fragments, lettres,* ed. Jérôme Peignot and the Collectif Change (Paris: Pauvert, 1977), 284. Bataille's message to Colette's mother, transmitted through Marcel Moré: "Si jamais on poussait l'audace jusqu'à célébrer une messe, il tirerait sur le prêtre à l'autel."

28. Patrick Waldberg and Isabelle Waldberg, *Un Amour Acéphale, correspondance 1940–49* (Paris: La Différence, 1992), 10.

29. Susan Rubin Suleiman, "Bataille in the Street: The Search for Virility in the 1930s," in *Bataille: Writing the Sacred,* ed. Carolyn Bailey Gill (London, Routledge, 1995), 39.

30. In French expression, **l'expérience intérieure** has usually been translated as "the interior experience." However, given Bataille's fascination with science and with pushing the limits of commonly accepted experiences, the translation of **expérience** as "experiment" is more pertinent to what he was attempting.

31. Surya (387, n. 3) effectively explains the influence of Socrates thus: "Le 'connais-toi toi-même' servirait à définir la possibilité de l'expérience

intérieure négative, et le 'je ne sais qu'une chose, c'est que je ne sais rien', le non-savoir approché et découvert par cette expérience."

32. *Ibid.*, 393, n. 1. Surya notes this sale, thus indicating that the text was written prior to the end of World War II.

33. Alain Arnaud and Gisèle Excoffon-Lafarge, *Bataille* (Paris: Seuil [Ecrivains de toujours]: 1978), 180, n. 1.

34. Madeline Chapsal, *Envoyez la petite musique* (Paris: Grasset, 1984), 236.

35. See Richardson, *Georges Bataille,* 120–22 and ff. for elaborations on the shaman motif in Bataille's work and as a model for his own role within the various groups he organized.

36. Jules Monnerot, *La Poésie moderne et le sacré* (Paris: Gallimard, 1945), 114.

37. Michèle Richman, "La Signification de la revue *Critique* dans l'oeuvre de Bataille," *Actes du colloque international d'Amsterdam, 21–22 June 1985* (Amsterdam: Rodopi, 1987), 132.

38. *Ibid.*, 142. Michèle Richman notes that Bataille himself admits that his exchange with Sartre precipitated a revision in his own thought.

39. Surya, 489: "celui-ci [Bataille] a toute sa vie manqué d'argent."

40. Bataille wrote in a copy of *L'Abbé C.* given to Jean Breton (*Un Bruit de Fête* [Paris: Cherche Midi, 1990], 74): "l'érotisme signifiait pour moi ce retour à l'unité, que la religion opère à froid." Bataille's concern with unity is likewise part of his vision for the links between communication and communion (OC, VII, 279). Note that "communion" is a Catholic ritual of which the priest is the consecrator, i.e., he is the one who makes the unity of communion "holy" within the Mass. Given such a role, the priest then offers the possibility to be a key for the unity of the secular interests of humanity. See entry for **prètre** in glossary.

41. Suleiman, "Bataille in the Streets," 43: "Rhetorically, 'virility' carries with it too much old baggage."

42. Bataille, *Eponine,* 7: "Ce qui m'attire dans un prêtre est bien sûr ce qui lui manque."

43. Ungar (258–62) develops Bataille's Heideggerian vision of the Lascaux drawings.

44. Georges Bataille in Marguerite Duras, "Bataille, Feydeau et Dieu," *France Observateur,* no. 396 (12 December 1957): 21. My translation.

45. Pierre Klossowski, *Un si funeste désir* (Paris: Gallimard, 1963), 126.

46. Georges Bataille, *Ma Mère* (Paris: Jean-Jacques Pauvert, 1966), 109.

47. Susan Rubin Suleiman explains Bataille's *Histoire de l'oeil* and much of his creative work with the insight that the mother's body is sacrificed for the son's life. See her "Transgression and the Avant-Garde: Bataille's *Histoire de l'oeil,*" in *On Bataille: Critical Essays,* ed. Leslie Anne Boldt-Irons (Albany: State University Press of New York, 1995), 313–33.

48. Maurice Blanchot, "L'Amitié," *Les Lettres nouvelles* 10 (new series), no. 29 (October 1962): 9.

*Chapter Two*

1. Daniel Hawley, *L'Oeuvre Insolite de Georges Bataille: Une hiérophanie moderne* (Geneva: Slatkine, 1978), 328.

2. Shadia B. Drury, *Alexandre Kojève: The Roots of Postmodern Politics* (New York: St. Martin's Press, 1994), 119: "Bataille's philosophical saga is from beginning to end a response to Kojève." Indeed, Bataille was strongly influenced by Kojève's orientation of Hegel. However, it is a question whether a single "philosophy" can be ascribed to Bataille. Bataille has too many inclinations to give the crucial position to Kojève.

3. Susan Sontag, *Styles of Radical Will* (New York: Dell, 1966), 60.

4. André Breton, "Second Manifeste du Surréalisme," in *Manifestes du surréalisme* (Paris: Jean-Jacques Pauvert, 1972), 149.

5. Surya (83) notes that Chestov presented a Pascalian Nietzsche and a "Nietzscheanized Pascal" in their mutual anguish over the abyss of faith.

6. Pierre Klossowski, in *Le Peintre et son démon: Entretiens avec Pierre Klossowski,* ed. Jean-Maurice Monnoyer (Paris: Gallimard, 1985), 177.

7. Jean-Louis Baudry in *Bataille,* ed. Philippe Sollers (Paris: V.G.E., 1973), 24: "Tout son livre sur Nietzsche indique une problématique morale, morale du sommet, morale du declin."

8. Weiss (132, n. 4): "Note that the community in question diminishes from that of a heterogeneous proletariat in *Contre-attack* [*sic*] to the secret community of Acéphale, finally to the isolation of the inner experience, where Bataille is in community with Nietzsche himself as described in the texts of *La somme athéologique*."

9. Annette Michelson, "Heterology and the Critique of Instrumental Reason," *October,* no. 36 (1986): 115.

10. Georges Bataille, *L'Abbé C.* (Paris: Minuit, 1950), 72.

11. Friedrich Nietzsche, *Thus Spake Zarathustra,* tr. Walter Kaufmann (New York: Penguin, 1966), 6 and 324.

12. Jean-Paul Sartre, *Situations,* vol. 1 (Paris: Gallimard, 1947), 170.

13. Jean-Michel Besnier, "Bataille, the Emotive Intellectual," tr. Alisdair McIntosh in Gill, 19.

14. Derrida (26 ff.) claims that sovereignty does not encompass the master because the master has had the strength to withstand the anguish of death and then to dominate the slave through the threat of death.

15. Georges Bataille, "Hegel, Death, and Sacrifice," tr. Jonathan Strauss, *Yale French Studies,* no. 78, ed. Allan Stoekl, (1990): 17, n. 6.

16. Jean-Michel Besnier, *La Politique de l'impossible: l'intellectuel entre révolte et engagement* (Paris: La Découverte, 1988), 51. My translation.

17. Maurice Blanchot, "La Littérature et le droit à la mort," in his *La Part du feu* (Paris: Gallimard, 1949), 319.

18. Derrida (pp. 31 ff.) notes that, following upon Bataille's Hegel, "on peut donc réinterpréter contre Hegel sa propre interprétation."

19. Michèle H. Richman, *Reading Georges Bataille: Beyond the Gift* (Baltimore: Johns Hopkins University Press, 1982), 47.

20. Michèle Richman, "Introduction to the Collège de Sociologie: Poststructuralism before its Time?", *Stanford French Studies* 12, no. 1 (Spring 1988): 84.

21. For discussions of these influences of Mauss, see my *Claude Lévi-Strauss* (Boston: Twayne World Author Series, 1987).

22. Jean Piel, "Bataille et le monde: De la 'Notion de dépense' à 'La Part maudite,' " *Critique: revue générale des publications françaises et étrangères,* no. 195–96 (August–September 1963), 725.

23. For a discussion of how this essay places a wedge within sociology that Bataille then opens into an elaboration of the place for a general economy, see Denis Hollier, "Malaise dans la sociologie," *L'Arc,* no. 48 (1972): 60 ff.

24. Marcel Mauss, *The Gift—The Form and Reason for Exchange in Archaic Societies,* tr. W. D. Halls (New York: W. W. Norton, 1990), 12: "To accept something from somebody is to accept some part of his [*sic*] spiritual essence, of his [*sic*] soul." It is the essence of gifts, once they are accepted, to "exert a magic or religious hold over you."

25. Michael Richardson (*The Absence of Myth,* 27, n. 22) observes this complete conformity of Bataille's sovereignty to Marx's early definition of communism as "the positive supersession of private property as human self-estrangement, and hence the true appropriation of the human essence through and for man" (cited from Marx's *Economic and Philosophical Manuscripts*).

26. Denis Hollier, "Bataille's Tomb: A Halloween Story," tr. Richard Miller, *October,* no. 33 (Summer 1985): 94.

27. Besnier, *La politique de l'impossible,* 127: "le souverain bataillien paraît bien solidaire des masses."

28. Max Weber, *The Protestant Ethic and the Spirit of Capitalism,* tr. Talcott Parsons (London: Harper Collins Academic, 1991), 105.

29. Steven Shaviro, *Passion and Excess: Blanchot, Bataille and Literary Theory* (Tallahassee: Florida State University Press, 1990), 106.

30. Miguel de Unamuno, *The Tragic Sense of Life in Men and Nations,* tr. Anthony Kerrigan (Princeton: Princeton University Press, 1972), 159.

*Chapter Three*

1. Denis Hollier, *La Prise de la Concorde* (Paris: Gallimard, 1974), 52. My translation.

2. Denis Hollier, "A Tale of Unsatisfied Desire," introduction to Georges Bataille, *Guilty,* tr. Bruce Boone (Venice, Calif.: Lapis Press, 1988), ix.

3. See Denis Hollier's argumentation (*Prise,* 52) about the imprisoning aspects of architecture as the counterpoint to Bataille's presentation of heterology: "l'écriture en ce sens sera un geste profondément anti-architectural. . . . "

4. Sylvère Lotringer, introduction to Georges Bataille, *On Nietzsche,* tr. Bruce Boone (New York: Paragon House, 1992), xi.

5. Philippe Sollers, "De grandes irrégularités de langage," *Critique,* no. 195–96 (1962): 796.

6. Yukio Mishima, "Essai sur Georges Bataille," tr. Tadao Takémoto and Michel Cazenave, *Nouvelle Revue Française,* no. 256 (April 1974): 79.

7. The Marquis de Sade's erotic writings can be seen as exemplifying the violence toward women that has the effect of making women disappear as players with men in the erotic community of humanity. Bataille is to be distinguished from Sade in this regard because, for Bataille, women do represent the Other for men such as himself and the alter egos of his narrators. Bataille does not want to erase them, as Sade's violence effectively does. Often, women become helpful as others to assist himself and his male narrators to understand themselves. On this point, I disagree with Richardson (*Absence,* 16) that Sade's and Bataille's writings were similarly provocative in this regard.

8. Georges Bataille, "The Sorcerer's Apprentice," in *The College of Sociology, 1937–39,* ed. Denis Hollier, tr. Betsy Wing (Minneapolis: University of Minnesota Press, 1988), 15.

9. For discussions of Bataille's fiction as "pornographic," see especially: Andrea Dworkin, *Pornography: Men Possessing Women* (New York: G. P. Putnam's Sons, 1979), 175 ff.; Susan Sontag, "The Pornographic Imagination," in her *Styles of Radical Will* (New York: Delta, 1981), 35–73; and Susan Rubin Suleiman, "Pornography, Transgression, and the Avant-Garde: Bataille's *Story of the Eye,*" in *The Poetics of Gender,* ed. Nancy K. Miller (New York: Columbia University Press, 1986), 117–36.

10. For a discussion of the nature of Bataille's challenge to the sacred as represented by the Church, capitalism, and fascism, see my "Bakhtin's Comic Dismemberment and the Pornography of Georges Bataille's 'Story of the Eye' (1928)," *Humor: International Journal of Humor Research* 3, no. 2 (Spring 1990): 177–91.

11. Susan Rubin Suleiman (in her "Pornography") analyzes *L'Histoire de l'oeil* as a "confrontation between an all-powerful father and a traumatized son, a confrontation staged across and over the body of the mother" (132).

12. Jean François Fourny, *Introduction à la lecture de Geroges Bataille* (New York: Peter Lang, 1988), 54.

13. Mark C. Taylor, *Altarity* (Chicago: University of Chicago Press, 1987), 124.

14. Lucette Finas, *La Crue: Une Lecture de Bataille: Madame Edwarda* (Paris: Gallimard, 1972), 141: "La bête n'est jamais nue: seule est nue la bête-en-l'homme, le sacré. La reconnaissance de bête (de la-bête-en-l'homme) est reconnaissance de dette."

15. Maurice Blanchot, *L'Entretien infini* (Paris: Gallimard, 1969), 300.

16. Surya, 539: *Madame Edwarda, Ma Mère,* and the unfinished *Charlotte d'Ingerville* were supposed to complete this trilogy.

17. Georges Bataille, "Letter to René Char on the Incompatibilities of the Writer," tr. Christopher Carsten, in *Yale French Studies,* no. 78, ed. Allan Stoekl (1990): 40.

18. Bataille and Michel Leiris were crucial in providing the notes for Laure, *Ecrits: fragments, lettres,* ed. Jérôme Peignot (Paris: Pauvert, 1977).

19. For a study of Bataille's insights into the image of the sun and its emasculating power in painting, see Briony Fer, "Poussière/Painting: Bataille on Painting," in Gill, 154–71.

20. Jean Piel, Bataille's friend since 1927, claims that *La Part Maudite* reveals a systematic philosophical vision that has a fourfold impact: as philosophy of nature, philosophy of humanity, economic philosophy, and the philosophy of history. See his article "Bataille et le monde: De la 'notion de dépense' à 'la part maudite,' " *Critique,* no. 195–96 (August–September 1963): 721–33.

21. Jean-Luc Nancy, "La Communauté désoeuvrée," *Alea* IV (1983): 15.

22. Martin Heidegger, *Being and Time,* tr. John Macquarrie and Edward Robinson (New York: Harper & Row, 1962), 377, section 329.

23. Rosalind Kraus, "Antivision," *October*, no. 36 (Spring 1986): 152.

24. Nicolas Calas, "Acephalic Mysticism," *Hemisphères* 2, no. 6 (1945): 6.

25. Rosalind Kraus, "Corpus Delicti," *October,* no. 33 (summer 1985): 39.

26. André Masson, "Some Notes on the Unusual Georges Bataille," *Art and Literature,* no. 3 (Autumn–Winter 1964): 111.

27. Some feminist readers may agree with Susan Rubin Suleiman (*Streets,* 43) when she notes that Bataille's "rhetoric of virility" is too conformist with unacceptable sexual politics. This is too blanket a condemnation of Bataille, who is not alone during the 1930s (note, for example, Malraux, Drieu la Rochelle, and Aragon) in espousing "virility" as a metaphor (albeit sexist) to speak of a human ideology of courage and integrity.

28. Pierre Mazara, " 'La Littérature est du côté du mal' explique Georges Bataille," *Le Figaro littéraire,* 12 October 1957, 12.

29. Joseph Libertson, "Bataille and Communication: From Heterogeneity to Continuity," *Modern Language Notes* 89, no. 4 (May 1974): 671.

30. For a developed presentation of this stance by Kojève, Blanchot, Marx, Hegel, Heidegger, and Bataille, see Besnier, *La Politique de l'impossible*.

31. Maurice Blanchot (1983, 27) claims that Bataille was actively involved in writing political tracts for *Contre-Attaque*.

32. In 1937, the secret society of Acéphale was composed of Georges Ambrosino, Henri Dubief, Georges Duthuit, Pierre Klossowski, Colette Peignot, Patrick Waldberg, and Bataille. After Colette's death in 1938, Isabelle Waldberg became a member of the group.

33. Georges Bataille, "La Littérature est-elle utile?", *Combat,* 12 November 1944, 1.

34. Allan Stoekl, "1937, March," in *A New History of French Literature,* ed. Denis Hollier (Cambridge: Harvard University Press, 1989), 932.

35. Joseph Libertson, *Proximity: Levinas, Blanchot, Bataille and Communication* (The Hague: Martinus Nijhoff), 113.

36. Denis Hollier, *Against Architecture: The Writings of Georges Bataille,* tr. Betsy Wing (Cambridge: MIT Press, 1989), ix–xxiii.

37. Denis Hollier, "Bloody Sundays," tr. Betsy Wing, *Representations* 28 (Fall 1989): 79.

38. Allan Stoekl, "Hegel's Return," *Stanford French Review* 12, no. 1 (Spring 1988): 128.

*Chapter Four*

1. See my *Philippe Sollers* (Amsterdam: Editions Rodopi, 1996) for a discussion of the interrelated arguments of Sollers's creative and theoretical works with Bataille's own.

2. See my *Jacques Derrida* (New York: Twayne World Author Series, 1995) for a presentation of the changing nature of Derrida's questions in his writings.

3. André Breton, *Manifestes du surréalisme* (Paris: Jean-Jacques Pauvert, 1972), 146.

4. Bataille did engage in considerable antisurrealist rhetoric. For example, he opposed Breton's leadership of what he called "the Surrealist religion" (OC, I, 218) by remarking as late as 1948 that ". . . Surrealism abandoned a certain equivocation, such that I have defined as being inherent to religion up until Christianity" (OC, VII, 381). Such "equivocation" Bataille finds necessary for his mystical vision of an atheological religious ritual.

5. See Georges Bataille, *The Absence of Myth: Writings on Surrealism,* ed. and tr. Michael Richardson (London: Verso, 1994) for collected texts by Bataille on surrealism as well as the introduction by Richardson developing Bataille's complex, evolving relationship with surrealism and with Breton himself.

6. Maurice Blanchot, *Faux pas* (Paris: Gallimard, 1943), 51–57.

7. Michel Foucault, "Préface à la transgression," *Critique,* no. 195–96 (August–September 1963): 751–69. Translated into English in Michel Foucault, *Language, Counter-Memory, Practice,* tr. Donald F. Bouchard and Sherry Simon (Ithaca, N.Y.: Cornell University Press, 1977), 29–52.

8. Roland Barthes, "La Métaphore de l'oeil," *Critique,* no. 195–96 (1962): 770–77. Translated by Richard Howard in Roland Barthes, *Critical Essays* (Evanston, Ill.: Northwestern University Press, 1972), 239–47.

9. For a discussion of how Barthes vilifies Bataille's symbolic order, see Michael Halley, "And a Truth for a Truth: Roland Barthes on Georges Bataille," *French Literature Series* 10 (1983): 113–22.

10. For a discussion of Bataille's *Madame Edwarda* as an aesthetic experience of the relationships between death and eroticism, see Sontag, 35–73.

11. Roland Barthes, "Les Sorties du texte," in Sollers, *Bataille,* 54.

12. For a discussion of the fragment or essay as the key to Barthes's intellectual endowment from Bataille (and others), see Réda Bensmaïa, *Barthes à l'essai: Introduction au texte réfléchissant* (Tübingen: Gunter Narr Verlag, 1986).

13. Michel Leiris notes the reaction of administrators within the BN as cited by Michel Surya, *Georges Bataille, la mort à l'oeuvre* (Paris: Gallimard, 1992), 183.

14. Note the following as the major essays by Philippe Sollers on Bataille: "De Grandes Irrégularités de langage," *Critique,* no. 195–96 (1962): 795–802; "Le Toit," *Tel Quel,* no. 29 (Spring 1967): 25–46; "La Grande Méthode," *Tel Quel,* no. 34 (Summer 1968): 21–27; "Le Récit impossible," in his *Logiques* (Paris: Seuil, 1968), 158–63; "Le Coupable," *Tel Quel,* no. 45 (Spring 1971): 97–100; and "Une Prophétie de Bataille," in his *La Guerre du goût* (Paris: Gallimard, 1994), 455–59.

15. Denis Hollier, "Le Materialisme dualiste de Georges Bataille," *Tel Quel,* no. 25 (Spring 1966): 42.

16. Bernard Sichère, "L'Écriture souveraine de Georges Bataille," *Tel Quel,* no. 93 (Autumn 1982): 63.

17. Jacques Derrida, *Margins of Philosophy,* tr. Alan Bass (Chicago: University of Chicago Press, 1982), 309.

18. Jürgen Habermas, "The French Path to Postmodernity: Bataille between Eroticism and General Economics," tr. Fredrick Lawrence, *New German Critique* 33 (1984): 90.

19. Jürgen Habermas, *The Philosophical Discourse of Modernity,* tr. Frederick Lawrence (Cambridge: MIT Press, 1987), 236.

20. Calas (5) notes that "from the point of view of a history of ideas Bataille's theories are interesting because they are an attempt to give a sociological and psychological foundation to those existentialist theories that have their origins in Schelling's philosophy."

21. Jean Baudrillard, "Quand Bataille attaquait le principe métaphysique de l'économie," *La Quinzaine Littéraire,* no. 234 (1–15 June 1976): 5. My translation. See the English translation of the entire review by David James Miller in *Canadian Journal of Political and Social Theory* 11, no. 3 (1987): 57–62.

22. Jean Baudrillard, *L'Échange symbolique et la mort* (Paris: Gallimard, 1976), 238.

23. Jean Baudrillard, *For a Critique of the Political Economy of the Sign,* tr. Charles Levin (St. Louis: Telos Press, 1981), 64.

24. Jean Baudrillard, *Cool Memories,* tr. Chris Turner (London: Verso, 1990), 143.

25. Jean-Luc Nancy, *La Communauté désoeuvrée* (Paris: Christian Bourgois, 1986), 50.

26. Nancy, *Alea,* 29: "Cependant, Bataille lui-même resta suspendu entre les deux pôles de l'extase et de la communauté."

27. Dominique de Roux, *Immédiatement* (Paris: Christian Bourgois, 1972), 147.

28. Benoîte Groult in *New French Feminisms,* ed. Elaine Marks and Isabelle de Courtivron (New York: Schocken, 1981), 70.

29. Anne-Marie Dardignan, *Les Chateaux d'Eros ou les infortunes du sexe des femmes* (Paris: François Maspero, 1981), 119.

30. Verena Andermatt Conley, *Hélène Cixous: Writing the Feminine* (Lincoln: University of Nebraska Press, 1984), 28. See also Lynn Penrod, *Hélène Cixous* (New York: Twayne, 1996), 22, 23, 65–66.

*Chapter Five*

1. Bernard-Henri Lévy, *Les Indes rouges* (Paris: Grasset et Librairie Générale Française, 1985), 93.

2. See my *Ethics of Reading According to Emmanuel Lévinas* (Amsterdam: Rodopi, 1999).

3. Marguerite Duras, "À propos de Georges Bataille," in her *Outside: Papers d'un jour* (Paris: Albin Michel, 1981), 34.

# *A Glossary of Bataille's Vocabulary*

Georges Bataille's struggle with vocabulary is part of his struggle for control over his existence. The following words are chosen from his complete works as words that have specifically unique usages for him. The first word is an approximate English translation of Bataille's concept.

**l'abîme**—The abyss is one of Bataille's favorite images expressing the anguish at the lacunae in heterology; B's visit to Mount Etna in Sicily gave him an experiential and materialistic vision of what he struggled with inside himself; part of B's fascination with emptiness (**le trou**, the hole; **le vide**, the empty space).

**s'abîmer**—To be lost in oneself; often describes B's fictional characters when they are overcome by their anguish.

**l'Acéphale**—Acephale is a headless god worshiped by chthonic religions and the symbol for B's study of subversion and discontinuity as religious experiences.

**l'angoisse**—Anguish is the experience of the continuity and the discontinuity of Being accompanied by the simultaneous lack of communication among humans; anguish is absolute sovereignty, according to the narrator of *Madame Edwarda,* and is produced by the experience of nothingness.

**l'anus**—The anus is an image of base materialism through which energy is released; it is the bodily equivalent to the volcano.

**l'architecture**—Architecture is part of the need to establish capitalist principles for hierarchical structuring in the human environment.

**l'athéologie**—Atheology is a negative theology, a theology without God,whereby the myth of the sacred becomes the organizing principle for the recognition of the continuity in life.

**l'aveu**—Confession is a function usually identified with language; it leads to anguish (see **angoisse**); the contrast to provocation.

**la boue**—Mud is that in which daily life struggles; this principle of base materialism (see **le matérialisme**) contrasts with the ecstasy of the inner experiment.

**la communauté**—Community is an ecstatic experience attained by individual beings working generously together with the sacred.

**la communication**—Communication is the solidarity achieved through generosity and expenditure that results from the recognition of the importance of community for the meditating subject.

**la charade**—The charade is the denial of communication with others; the priest (see **le prêtre**) exemplifies this human trait.

**la contestation**—Confrontation is the testing of the limits of thought and Being to define their nature; it typically has a political overtone referring to the subversion of limits or dominant ideologies, e.g., used in B's reappreciation of surrealism after World War II as opposed to the "servile" utility of Sartre's call for a "committed" writer and literature.

**la continuité**—Continuity is the experience of Being.

**la cruauté**—Cruelty is an act of sovereinty and a voluntary withdrawal from communication with others.

**le criminel**—The criminal is the sovereign (see **souveraineté**) who understands that transgression and taboo constitute one of the crucial paradoxes of Being.

**dénuder**—Revealing, as if beyond a mask, what was previously hidden.

**la dépense**—Expenditure, also loss, is contrasted with accumulation, utility, and profit as the major principle of a general (rather than a specific) economy; through its practice, expenditure is identified with violence and the transgression of conservation and homogeneity to provide the means for surplus value as the instrument of generosity.

**la dialectique**—The dialectic of Hegel was learned by B. through Kojève to be the master-slave relation whereby the negative (the slave) always subverts the authority of the hierarchy (the master).

**Dieu**—God is a manifestation of the sacred for some organized religions (especially Christianity), but it is an idealistic concept important for contrasting with dialectical materialism.

**la discontinuité**—Discontinuity is opposed to continuity and is achieved by the transgression of the sacred.

**le divin**—The divine is the experience of what is outside of the world (**hors du monde**: *L'Abbé C.*).

**l'économie générale**—The general economy is an elaborate alternative to various kinds of restricted economy and implements the principle of the expenditure of surplus value without compensation rather than the accumulation fostered by bourgeois and Reform Christian ideologies.

**l'énigme**—The enigma is the need to pose teleological questions that cannot be answered as a way of avoiding the discontinuity of Death.

**L'Erotisme**—Eroticism is called the "problem of problems" by B.; it is participation in the continuity (life) and discontinuity (death) of Being, taboo and transgression, and religion and the inner experiment.

**l'Etre**—Being is the ultimate experience of continuity with life and Death.

**l'excédent**—The surplus of energy and wealth in the universe proposed by B. to be expended rather than saved or reinvested for useful purposes.

**l'excès**—Overindulgence is the violent thinking of the unthinkable.

**l'expérience intérieure**—The inner experiment is a term preferred to mysticism by which the subject reflects internally to find the common bond of being, a communication with the community of others.

**l'extase**—Ecstasy is the vision and joy that can be attained through the practice of one's inner experiment with the sacred.

**la fascination**—Fascination is the temporary looking away from the anguish of nothingness.

**la forêt**—The forest is a sacrosanct place where B.'s fictional characters experience the secret sensuality of their bodies (e.g., *L'Histoire de l'oeil*; *Ma Mère*; and *Charlotte d'Ingerville*), usually regarded as shameful in society.

**la générosité**—Generosity is the recognition of the importance of the community to the individual who shares surplus value with others.

**le glissement**—The slippery nature of boundaries separating limits (see **l'interdit**) from their transgression (see **la transgression**).

**le gnosis**—Mysterious knowledge attained through spiritual experience.

**l'hétérologie**—Heterology is ambivalence that is at the core of identity and the basic principle of materialism that cannot be appropriated or assimilated; sometimes called **scatologie** (scatology).

**l'homme entier**—The total human is contrasted with the "man of action" who is politically and socially involved in a community; this person meditates on the involvement and does not respect a hierarchical relationship between action and mysticism.

**l'horreur**—Horror is the personal anguish of the experience of nothingness.

**l'idéalisme**—Idealism is a teleological experience of the continuity of life.

**l'impossible**—The impossible is the experience of evading the limits imposed by taboo.

**l'impuissance**—Impotence is an anxiety that is inwardly directed and incapable of active sexual, political, and moral energy, e.g., Troppmann in *Le Bleu du ciel*; opposed to **virilité** (virility).

**l'informe**—Formlessness that transgresses while affirming the limitations of concepts in their abstractness and self-assurance.

**l'interdit**—Taboo is a necessary construct of a community to acquaint a meditating subject with the continuity of Being; it is the necessary correlative to transgression (see **la transgression**).

**la jouissance**—Orgasm as a metaphor for the ultimate pleasures of eroticism and death.

**le manque**—Lack that is the basis for desire, orgasm (**jouissance**), and anguish as Heidegger's experience of nothingness.

**le matérialisme**—Base materialism is a religious and psychological validation of what is usually referred to as "waste" within idealism; base materialism is heterogeneous by its nature and therefore not totalizable.

**méduser**—Staring or gazing that reveals the continuity and discontinuity of Being and Death.

**mettre en jeu**—Calling into question is what must be constantly done to refuse the programming of idealist thinking and to place one in the communication of communion; this term is identified by Jacques Derrida as one of the fundamental and most frequent expressions used by B.

**la mort**—Death is the final discontinuity that gives a sense of limits to the continuity of life and leads to an appreciation of the sense of community.

**le mysticisme**—Mysticism is the practice of obscene (see **l'obscénité**) visions of transgression and the subversion of hierarchical structure.

**le mythe**—Myth is the ritual practiced by a community to celebrate what it considers to be sacred.

**le non-savoir**—Nonknowledge is the recognition of the limitations of knowledge; it is the nexus for the study of laughter, tears, the sacred, poetry, anguish, and ecstasy.

**la nudité**—Nudity is an index of human vulnerability (see **vulnérabilité**) and exposes human participation in animal (but animals themselves cannot be naked) and divine (i.e., the mystical desire inspired by nudity) nature (e.g., *Madame Edwarda*).

**la nuit**—Night is emptiness and reflects the void of inner anguish.

**l'obscénité**—Obscenity is the focal point of mysticism by which the subject transgresses the taboo (see **l'interdit**) of a community (e.g., *Le Mort*); it has the ambivalent power of bringing some to orgasm and to make others laugh.

**l'oeil**—The eye is the organ of the body that does not see as well as the ecstatic vision.

**l'oeil pinéal**—The prickly eye is the human embodiment of the sun's energy; it is the combination of a sexual gland (**pine** meaning "prick") and ecstatic vision.

**le petit mort**—"The endearing dead one" is an idiomatic expression for orgasm, thus portraying erotic life in imitation of death.

**le potlatch**—Potlatch is the gift that is the basis for exchange and communication in communities studied by Marcel Mauss; it provides B. with the anthropological basis for his theory of the general economy.

**le pouvoir**—Power is the sovereignty (see **souveraineté**) of the individual subject to act without idealist parameters.

**le prêtre**—The priest is an idealist monster because, within Catholicism, he denies the value of eroticism for himself.

**la provocation**—Provocation of the Other into being alive is the highest function of language in opposition to confession (cf. **l'aveu**).

**le rire**—Laughter is learned from Nietzsche as the only appropriate reaction to the paradoxes of Being.

**risible**—Laughable is the condition of the hilarious (**l'hilarité**) paradoxes of Being; e.g., human nature is laughable.

**le sacré**—The sacred is taken from Durkheim as the abstract unity of a social unit; B. identifies this word with communication and community; it was studied by the Collège de Sociologie and attracted sociological studies by Caillois, Monnerot, and others. From *sacer,* meaning "defiled" and "holy."

**le sacrifice**—Sacrifice is a religious cult linking eroticism and death in an experience of taboo and trangression; the Catholic Mass is the site for the symbolic reenactment of this practice by other religions united in community by their respect for the sacred purpose of murdering another.

**le sacrilège**—Sacrilege is a crime against society's propagation of what is sacred.

**le savoir**—Knowledge is contrasted with nonknowledge (**le non-savoir**) as a quantitative task that science accumulates; the Kinsey Report is an example of the link between science and knowledge.

**le scandale**—Scandal is the provocation of society; a positive challenge to bourgeois idealism; often found as **scandaleux** (scandalous), and the verb **scandaliser** (to scandalize).

**la scatologie**—Scatology is base materialism that cannot be assimilated or appropriated; the opposite of idealism; also referred to as **hétérologie** (heterology).

**la scissiparité**—Schizogenesis, the process of internal cellular division, is a biological model for the social ambiguities of the relationships between being and community, anguish and communication.

**le silence**—The silence of death is contrasted with the loquacious state of language in life.

**la société**—Society is a compound being that is more than the sum of its parts.

**le soleil**—The sun is the model for absolute expenditure because of its outpouring of energy in the universe.

**souiller**—To dirty is to bring recognition that life's struggles are with the components of base materialism; the character Dirty in *Le Bleu du ciel* is the incarnation of this principle.

**la souveraineté**—Sovereignty is the subject's independence to perform gratuitous acts without teleological purpose; cf. **l'utilité** (utility).

**la torture**—Torture as a means used to make people talk, denounce others, experience agony; nevertheless, some resist heroically (the Abbé C.); cf. B.'s psychoanalysis with Adrien Borel.

**la totalisation**—Totalizing is an idealistic enterprise of homogeneity (cf. **la dépense**); it is characteristic of sovereignty and is linked with Sade's vision of **l'homme entier.**

**la transgression**—Transgression is the correlative of taboo (see **l'interdit**); they are in a necessary relationship; to transgress limits is to affirm the existence of those very limits.

**le trou**—The abyss of anguish is the human solitude and emptiness as if before death itself; also expressed as **le gouffre**, **l'abîme**, and **le vide.**

**l'utilité**—The usefulness of savings or reinvestments that capitalism and Reform Christianity favors regarding the surplus of wealth; opposed to **souveraineté** (sovereignty).

**le vide**—The emptiness of anguish is experienced as the ultimate solitude of the individual facing death and its preludes (eroticism; ecstatic vision; solitude); also called **l'abîme**, **le gouffre**, and **le trou.**

**la virilité**—Virility is a sexual, political, and moral condition that emphasizes an active, emotive involvement in history; a sexist category that is opposed to l'**impuissance** (impotence).

**la vision intérieure**—The interior vision is the only valid religion for B.

**le volcan**—The volcano is a source of pent-up energy, always threatening to explode and follow its natural course of expenditure.

**la vulnérabilité**—Vulnerability is the tendency toward closure in that which lacks nothing as in the experience of **nudité** (nudity).

# *Selected Bibliography*

## PRIMARY SOURCES


### *Oeuvres complètes*, volumes I–XII. Paris: Gallimard.

Volume I. *Premiers Ecrits, 1922–1940. Histoire de l'oeil. L'Anus solaire. Sacrifices. Articles*. Ed. Denis Hollier. 1970.

Volume II. *Ecrits posthumes, 1922–1940.* Ed. Denis Hollier. 1970.

Volume III. *Oeuvres littéraires. Madame Edwarda. Le Petit. L'Archangélique. L'Impossible. La Scissiparité. L'Abbé C. L'Etre indifférencié n'est rien. Le Bleu du ciel*. Ed. Thadée Klossowski. 1971.

Volume IV. *Oeuvres littéraires posthumes. Poèmes. Le Mort. Julie. La Maison brûlée. La Tombe de Louis XXX. Divinus Deus. Ebauches*. Ed. Thadée Klossowski. 1971.

Volume V. *La Somme athéologique, I. L'Expérience intérieure. Méthode de méditation. Post-scriptum, 1953. Le Coupable. L'Alleluiah: Catéchisme de Dianus*. Ed. Paule Leduc. 1973.

Volume VI. *La Somme athéologique, II. Sur Nietzsche. Mémorandum. Annexes*. Ed. Henri Ronse and Jean-Michel Rey. 1973.

Volume VII. *L'Economie à la mesure de l'univers. La Part Maudite, I. La Limite de l'utile. Théorie de la religion. Conférences, 1947–1948. Annexes*. Ed. Thadée Klossowski. 1976.

Volume VIII. *L'Histoire de l'érotisme. Le Surréalisme au jour le jour. Conférences, 1951–1953. La Souveraineté. Annexes*. Ed. Thadée Klossowski. 1976.

Volume IX. *Lascaux. Manet. La Littérature et le mal. Dossier de Lascaux. Dossier William Blake*. Ed. Denis Hollier. 1979.

Volume X. *L'Érotisme. Le Procès de Gilles de Rais. Les Larmes d'Éros. Dossier de l'Érotisme. Dossier des Larmes d'Éros. Hors Les Larmes d'Éros*. Ed. Francis Marmande and Yves Thévenieau. 1987.

Volume XI. *Articles, I. 1944–1949*. Ed. Francis Marmande and Sibylle Monod. 1988.

Volume XII. *Articles, II. 1949–1961*. Ed. Francis Marmande and Sibylle Monod. 1988.

### Translations of Bataille's Work

*The Absence of Myth*. Tr. Michael Richardson. London: Verso, 1994.

*The Accursed Share*. Tr. Robert Hurley. New York: Zone Books. Vol. 1, 1988. Vol. 2 and 3, 1991.

*The Bataille Reader.* Ed. Fred Botting and Scott Wilson. Boston and Oxford: Blackwell, 1997.
The *Beast at Heaven's Gate*. Tr. Austryn Wainhouse. Paris: Olympia Press, 1956.
*Blue of Noon*. Tr. Harry Matthews. London: Boyars, 1979.
*The College of Sociology, 1937–39*. Ed. Denis Hollier. Tr. Betsy Wing. Minneapolis: University of Minnesota Press, 1988.
*Death and Sensuality: A Study of Eroticism and Taboo*. New York: Walker and Co., 1962. Arnos Press reprint, 1977.
*Encyclopaedia Acephalica*. Ed. Georges Bataille. Tr. Iain White et al. London: Atlas Press, 1995.
*Erotism: Death and Sensuality*. Tr. Mary Dalwood. San Francisco: City Lights, 1986.
*Guilty*. Tr. Bruce Boone. Venice, Calif.: Lapis Press, 1988.
*The Impossible*. Tr. Robert Hurley. San Francisco: City Lights, 1991.
*Inner Experience*. Tr. Leslie Anne Boldt. Albany: State University of New York Press, 1988.
*L'Abbé C*. Tr. Philip A. Facey. New York: Boyars, 1989.
*Literature and Evil*. Tr. Alastair Hamilton. New York: Boyars, 1993.
*Manet*. Trs. Austryn Wainhouse and James Emmons. Geneva: Skira, 1955.
*My Mother*. Tr. Austryn Wainhouse. Paris: Olympia Press, 1956.
*My Mother, Madame Edwarda, The Dead Man*. Tr. Austryn Wainhouse. London: Boyars, 1989.
*October* 36 (Spring 1986). Twenty-one various essays by B.
*On Nietzsche*. Tr. Bruce Boone with introduction by Sylvère Lotringer. New York: Paragon, 1992.
*Prehistoric Paintings: Lascaux or the Birth of Art*. Tr. Austryn Wainhouse. Geneva: Skira, 1955.
*Story of the Eye*. Tr. Joachim Neugroschel. San Francisco: City Lights, 1987.
*The Tears of Eros*. Tr. Peter Connor. San Francisco: City Lights, 1989.
*Theory of Religion*. Tr. Robert Hurley. New York: Zone Books, 1992.
*The Trial of Gilles de Rais*. Tr. Robert Robinson. Los Angeles: Amok, 1991.
*Visions of Excess: Selected Writings, 1927–1939*. Tr. Allan Stoekl. Minneapolis: University of Minnesota Press, 1985.

### Correspondence

*Lettres à Roger Caillois*. Ed. Jean-Pierre Le Bouler. Rennes: Editions Folle Avoine, 1987.

### Journals and Contributions by Bataille Reissued

*Acéphale: Religion, Sociologie, Philosophie*. 1936–1939. Ed. Michel Camus. Paris: Jean-Michel Place, 1980.
*Le Collège de Sociologie, 1937–1938*. Ed. Denis Hollier. Paris: Idées/Gallimard, 1979.

*La Critique sociale*. Preface by Boris Souvarine. Paris: Edtions de la Différence, 1983.
*Documents; Doctrines, Archéologie, Beaux-Arts, Ethnographie*. Ed. Bernard Noël. Paris: Mercure de France, 1968.
*Documents*. Vol. 1, 1929. Preface by Denis Hollier. Paris: Jean-Michel Place, 1992.
*Documents*. Vol. 2, 1930. Paris: Jean-Michel Place, 1992.
*L'Affaire Sade*. Paris: Jean-Jacques Pauvert, 1957.

### Works Edited by Bataille

Laure (Colette Peignot). *Le Sacré, suivi de Poèmes et de Divers Ecrits*. Ed. with Michel Leiris. Paris: Hors Commerce, 1939. Reprinted in *Ecrits de Laure,* Paris: Jean-Jacques Pauvert, 1971.
———. *Histoire d'une petite fille*. Ed. with Michel Leiris. Paris: Hors Commerce, 1943.
*Procès de Gille de Rais*. Ed. with Pierre Klossowski. Paris: Club Français du Livre, 1959.

### Translation by Bataille

Chestov, Léon. *L'idée de bien chez Tolstoi et Nietzsche (philosophie et prédication)*. Tr. from Russian by T. Beresovski-Chestov and Georges Bataille. Paris: Editions du Siècle, 1925.

### Bibliographies of Bataille's Work

*L'Arc*, no. 32 (1967): 92–96. Special issue on B.
*Critique,* no. 195–96 (August–September 1963), 804–32. Special issue on B.
Hawley, Daniel. *Bibliographie annotée de la critique sur Georges Bataille de 1929 à 1975*. Geneva: Droz, 1972.
Richman, Michèle. "Georges Bataille." In *Bibliography of 20th Century French Literature,* ed. Richard Brooks and Douglas Alden. Syracuse, N.Y.: Syracuse University Press, 1980, pp. 1437–40.
*Semiotexte* 2, no. 2 (1976).
Surya, Michel. *Georges Bataille, la mort à l'oeuvre*. Rev. ed. Paris: Gallimard, 1992, 689–97. A thorough listing of primary and secondary references until 1990.

## SECONDARY SOURCES

Finas, Lucette. *La Crue: Une Lecture de Bataille: Madame Edwarda*. Paris: Gallimard, 1972. Text and tables offering a close reading of *Madame Edwarda* with insights and expansions from other works by B.

Guerlac, Suzanne. *Literary Polemics: Bataille, Sartre, Valéry, Breton.* Stanford: Stanford University Press, 1997. Inspired reading of the nature of transgression in B.

Hollier, Denis. "Bataille's Tomb: A Halloween Story." Tr. Richard Miller. *October,* no. 33 (Summer 1985): 74–102. An inspired reading of necrophilia and the Don Juan syndrome throughout B.'s writings. *Bleu du ciel* presented as a political novel advocating communism.

———, ed. *The College of Sociology (1937–39)*. Tr. Betsy Wing. Minnesota: University of Minnesota Press, 1988. Crucial details about the events and lectures sponsored by Caillois and Bataille's *Collège de Sociologie.* This translation adds details and events not found in the 1979 French version.

LeBouler, Jean-Pierre, ed. *Lettres {de Georges Bataille} à Roger Caillois: 4 août 1935–4 février 1959*. Paris: Folle Avoine, 1987. Important details about the daily functioning of the *Collège de Sociologie* and how the relationship of Caillois and Bataille was crucial to the involvement of the major European intellectuals at the time. Francis Marmande contributes a foreword that gives an illuminating historical context for the correspondence.

LeBrun, Annie. *Soudain un bloc d'abîme, Sade*. Paris: Jean-Jacques Pauvert, 1986. Sovereignty is different in Bataille and in Sade. Sade's atheism, materialism, and denials of death and community are counterposed to Bataille's religion and the crucial roles of death and community. Cf. Richardson's introduction for critique.

Nancy, Jean-Luc. "La Communauté désoeuvrée." *Alea* 4 (1983): 11–48. Bataille's focus on communication is polarized between ecstasy and community. A community is the ecstatic communication of individual beings. Blanchot's term "la communauté désoeuvrée" is then realized in B.'s "sacred."

*October,* no. 36 (Autumn 1986). Special issue devoted to Georges Bataille. 21 essays by Bataille translated into English. Annette Michelson contributes an essay ("Heterology and the Critique of Instrumental Reason," 111–28) distinguishing Durkheim, Mauss, and Bataille with insights into Bataille, Adorno, and Horkheimer. Allen Weiss ("Impossible Sovereignty," 126–46) discusses the influence of Nietzsche on Bataille and the differences between the two.

Richardson, Michael. *Georges Bataille*. London and New York: Routledge, 1994. The postmodern appropriation of Bataille is wrong. Bataille is a sociologist who is often inconsistent but who affirms the paradoxes of life. Insights into Bataille as a shaman. Despite numerous editing problems, this is a reliable, balanced overview of Bataille's life and opus as products of a paradoxical vision, not merely focused on excess. Limited by a reluctance to admit Bataille's literary genius.

———. Introduction to his translation of Georges Bataille, *The Absence of Myth*. London: Verso, 1994. Bataille is a surrealist despite his critiques of surrealism. Bataille is closer to Breton than Sollers et al. portray them. Helpful distinctions between Bataille and Sade. Myth is a crucial concern for Bataille's thought.

Suleiman, Susan Rubin. "Bataille in the Street: The Search for Virility." In *Bataille: Writing the Sacred,* ed. Carolyn Bailey Gill. London: Routledge, 1995, 26–45. Historically grounded reading of Bataille's preoccupation with impotence. Virility is a moral, political, and sexual virtue in Bataille's works, esp. *Le Bleu du ciel*. These point toward the inward turn of Bataille's thought around 1937 to 1939.

———. "Pornography, Transgression, and the Avant-Garde." In *The Poetics of Gender,* ed. Nancy K. Miller. New York: Columbia University Press, 1986, 117–36. Feminist reading of Bataille's first erotic publication.

Surya, Michel. *Georges Bataille, la mort à l'oeuvre*. Rev. ed. Paris: Gallimard, 1992. Personal interviews, unpublished letters, and photographs from private collections provide unusual documents for a detailed life of Bataille and some insights into the relationships between his life and writings, despite a chatty and repetitive style. The first edition won the 1987 Prix Goncourt for biography. Good bibliography.

*Yale French Studies*, no. 78 (1990), ed. Allan Stoekl. Special issue on Bataille. Suzanne Guerlac offers a woman's perspective on Bataille. Two of Bataille's texts are translated: an essay on Kojève and Hegel and a letter to René Char on the incompatibilities of the writer. Allan Stoekl on Bataille's fascism and Steven Ungar on Bataille's interests in art are noteworthy.

# Index

## *The Author*

Roland A. Champagne is professor of French and chair of the Department of Foreign Languages and Literatures at the University of Missouri–St. Louis. He is the author of *Jacques Derrida* (1995), *The Structuralists on Myth* (1992), *French Structuralism* (1990), *Claude Lévi-Strauss* (1987), *Literary History in the Wake of Roland Barthes* (1984), and *Beyond the Structuralist Myth of Ecriture* (1977). His interests in aesthetics and ethics in contemporary literary theory have led to over 40 essays on Marguerite Duras, Maurice Blanchot, Philippe Sollers, Julia Kristeva, and Emmanuel Lévinas, published in such diverse journals as *SubStance, The French Review, New Literary History,* and *The American Journal of Semiotics,* among others.

## *The Editor*

David O'Connell is professor of French at Georgia State University. He received his Ph.D. in 1966 from Princeton University, where he was a National Woodrow Wilson Fellow, the Bergen Fellow in Romance Languages, and a National Woodrow Wilson Dissertation Fellow. He is the author of *The Teachings of Saint Louis: A Critical Text* (1972), *Les Propos de Saint Louis* (1974), *Louis-Ferdinand Céline* (1976), *The Instructions of Saint Louis: A Critical Text* (1979), and *Michel de Saint Pierre: A Catholic Novelist at the Crossroads* (1990). He has edited more than 60 books in the Twayne World Authors Series.